This book should be read by every[ ] [ ]dent and church associate pastor in America. Billy Hornsby knows what he is writing about. He has witnessed and experienced just about every angle on the leadership journey. Billy is a major strategist and facilitator for EQUIP's Million Leaders Mandate in Europe.

—JOHN C. MAXWELL
BEST-SELLING AUTHOR AND FOUNDER
OF THE INJOY GROUP

Success for the Second in Command offers a practical and applicable look at leadership for the second in command. Billy has captured a concept that is rarely taught but is extremely important for any organization to be successful.

—JOYCE MEYER
BEST-SELLING AUTHOR AND BIBLE TEACHER

Billy Hornsby gets to the heart of every subordinate leader's secret struggle to serve faithfully and fulfill his own sense of calling. Billy is a proven master at developing the leaders around him, and now the rest of us get to benefit from his wisdom, too. The sound Bible teaching and practical coaching in this book are a road map for every associate who has asked in his heart of hearts, "How do I make my mark?" This book will help you and your staff.

—TED HAGGARD
SENIOR PASTOR, NEW LIFE CHURCH

Billy Hornsby has a unique insight into the role of the second in command. He sees it as a calling and not a stepping-stone, and has taught me much while serving in that role in our church. He knows about influence and how to use it for the advantage of the organization, regardless of where you find yourself on the organizational chart. Thank you, friend, for a great book that will hopefully help many in finding their place and accomplishing their dream.

—GREG SURRATT
SENIOR PASTOR, SEACOAST CHURCH

Success for the Second of Command is a wealth of wisdom and information born out of practical experience. Billy understands the heart and the hurt of subordinate leaders and is a friend to everyone who leads from the second chair. It is a must read for every level of leadership.

—Chris Hodges
Senior Pastor, Church of the Highlands
Birmingham, Alabama

SUCCESS *for* THE SECOND *in* COMMAND

BILLY HORNSBY

CREATION HOUSE

A STRANG COMPANY

Success for the Second in Command by Billy Hornsby
Published by Creation House
A Strang Company
600 Rinehart Road
Lake Mary, Florida 32746
www.creationhouse.com

All Scripture quotations are from the New American Standard Bible. Copyright © 1960, 1962, 1963, 1968, 1971, 1972, 1973, 1975, 1977 by the Lockman Foundation. Used by permission. (www.Lockman.org)

This book was previously published by ARC Books, ISBN 0-9721195-2-3, copyright © 2004.

Cover design by Keith Neely, NDesign, Inc.

Library of Congress Control Number: 2005932819
International Standard Book Number: 1-59185-922-0

05 06 07 08 09 — 987654321
Printed in the United States of America

Contents

Foreword

IT HAS BEEN said that an institution is the lengthening shadow of a visionary leader. What rarely is said is that in the shadow of that visionary leader was *another* leader who executed the primary leader's ideas, monitored the budgets, built the infrastructure and systems, and, along the way, cleaned up a few of the messes. Such is the life of a leader who is "second in command."

For twenty years, I was my own boss. Oh, there were boards and congregations to whom I reported and was held accountable, but when it came to the directional and visionary aspects of leading organizations, it was clear to most that I was the guy in charge.

However, in early 2000, I made a significant career change by choice. I went from being "first in command" to "second in command." I went from being the first man to the second man. I went from being a shadow maker who cast vision and encouraged the masses, to the leader who lingered in the shadow of the visionary leader.

For me, moving from first to second, from senior to associate, was not as difficult as it has been for some. It helped that I made the change by design. But I won't kid with you—the change did require some significant adjustments on my part. There were some days, early in my transition, where I struggled with my new assignment, longed for the days of being "Number 1," missed the compliments, and craved the attention I once had.

It was in this season of change, still certain of God's call for me to be "second in command," that I began to evaluate the enormous advantages of my new and distinct place of leadership.

Yes, I said *leadership*. As the days became weeks and turned into months, I began to get a clearer understanding of the significant place God had given me as "Number 2." In my new role as the second in command, I was connecting and influencing more people in just a year than I ever did when I was "Number 1." My new boss's influence had given me a larger platform to develop my gifts to influence more lives, to make more friends, to raise more funds, to train more leaders, and to partner with more organizations and movements than I had ever experienced being my own boss.

Just a few years ago, the author of this book, Billy Hornsby, and I became friends. It wasn't too long after our first meeting that he began to share with me the idea of a book that would help to crystallize what it meant to be second in command in an organization. I encouraged Billy to write as much as he could about the unique blessings and advantages that come to those who follow their leaders in the "second chair" of their organizations.

In this book, Billy looks at some of the second-in-command leaders whose legacies outlived the legacies of their first-in-command leaders. Just think of it; in the Bible, some of the great heroes of the faith weren't the top positional persons in their arenas of life or occupation. Joseph led from the second chair. So did Daniel. So did Nehemiah. However, all these men led—and led well. They mobilized, related, negotiated, problem-solved, casted vision, and trusted God—and they influenced their nations for God's glory.

Billy does a great job of making the case that being "second" is as strategically and tactically important as being "first." In fact, if you were to look back on the some of the world's greatest and most lasting shadow-casters, and then look over their shoulders, you would see in their shadows some loyal, faithful, and secure individuals who were committed to carrying the vision of the primary leader in tough meetings or faraway lands.

If God has called you to be second in command, this book will serve as a resource to help you navigate through some occupational challenges and hazards. If God has called you to be the primary leader, this book will help you better understand those around you—those who daily are adding value to your life and work. Or, if you're second in command and are preparing to be first, or as I was, the first guy who was called to become the second guy, this book is for you.

Billy Hornsby comes alongside all leaders from the middle to the rear of the pack, gives them a hug, and reminds them that serving in the shadowlands of the primary leader is an attractive piece of real estate!

—JOHN D. HULL
PRESIDENT, EQUIP

Introduction

Pharaoh said to Joseph, "See I have set you over all the land of Egypt." Then Pharaoh took off his signet ring from his hand, and put it on Joseph's hand, and clothed him in garments of fine linen, and put the gold necklace around his neck. He had him ride in his second chariot.

—GENESIS 41:41–43

VICE PRESIDENT, ASSISTANT manager, associate pastor, personal assistant, co-captain, and many other terms like these express positions in leadership that, though subordinate, are indispensable in the success structures of business, industry, the military, and nonprofit organizations around the world. Often looked at as "not at the top yet," these can be positions where people enjoy long tenures of success and fulfillment.

It is my hope that this book will give you insights on how to choose, motivate, and appreciate the role of subordinate leaders and managers in your organization. Whether you lead from the number one position or from some lower rung on the organizational chart, you will benefit from the knowledge you will gather from the pages that follow. Get ready to realize your dream—no matter what position you are in right now.

1

Can any dream of greatness be realized from serving in the number two, number three, or number four spot? How do the vast majority of subordinate leaders in the world ever reach significance? How do they accomplish the vision that burns in their hearts when they are relegated to a lesser leadership position? I hope to answer these questions in this book.

See if you can find yourself in any of the scenarios below or if you've found yourself in a similar situation.

GIFTS ON HOLD

The position of department head had been vacated three different times as the previous department heads were promoted to supervisor. Rachel had served as the interim department head each time but was overlooked when a permanent replacement was found. In every case, one of her peers was promoted ahead of her to fill the job. Now it finally happened. She got the job. Rachel could now show the president of the company how gifted she was and what an asset she could be to the company.

In the first three management team meetings, she shared her creative ideas, ideas that she knew would make a positive impact on the company and ideas that surely her boss would be ready to implement immediately.

Rachel's ideas were rejected and status quo ruled the day. As her ideas were shelved time after time, meeting after meeting, her frustration began to mount. Rachel came to realize that the company didn't want her ideas, just her management skills and organizational savvy.

But what about her gifts? She had so much to offer, and the company was using only a small part of who she was and what she possessed inside.

Years passed, and nothing changed. Frustration has made Rachel bitter, and she functions at just a small percentage of her potential. Being a subordinate in a company with no vision for creativity and change has robbed her of expressing her gifts and realizing her potential for success. What should she do now?

Why? Don't You Trust Me?

Raymond has served as the right-hand man for Flow-Link Enterprises for fifteen years and has been given the responsibility to lead marketing and sales. But every time he makes a decision, the owner, Mr. Laethem, comes behind him and second-guesses those decisions.

After fifteen years, Raymond is completely equipped to handle his position and make the hard decisions that are required to keep the company successful and to meet all future goals. If the boss didn't trust him, then why did he give Raymond the responsibility? Why does the boss always have a better idea? Why can't he just trust the wisdom and experience of his best and longest-serving employee?

All Too Familiar

The scenarios above are just the tip of the iceberg in the lives of subordinate leaders in companies and organizations around the globe. Each is a peek into the life of a second in command, an assistant, the new kid on the block, or a trusted employee who is trying to find purpose and significance in life but seems to be held up by those above him on the leadership ladder. These are only two common maladies that seem to plague subordinate leaders who are trying to reach their potential in a world of extreme competition and self-interest.

Perhaps the story that follows, and the ensuing chapters of this book, will open your eyes to the possibilities that exist for you and anyone else who finds himself or herself trying to lead from the second, third, or fourth position in their company.

From this story taken from the life of Joseph, the son of the great Hebrew patriarch Jacob, we can discover how impossible dreams come true for faithful and loyal subordinates when they understand their role in the fulfillment of

those dreams. Below is a short version of one of the greatest
Bible stories.

THE STORY OF JOSEPH

Joseph, a shepherd, was the second youngest of the twelve sons
of Jacob. He was favored of his father and was given a coat of
many colors, which enraged his brothers. At the age of seventeen, Joseph brought bad reports of his brothers to his father.
But of himself he had dreams of becoming great—dreams he
could not understand. "We were binding sheaves in the field
and my sheaf stood up erect, and your sheaves bowed down
to my sheaf," he told his brothers. "The sun and the moon and
eleven stars were bowing down to me." With this proclama-
tion, hatred brewed deep in the hearts of his brothers. They
looked for the day when they could do away with Joseph.

It happened that Joseph was sent to look for his brothers
one day while they were watering the flocks. When they saw
him coming, they contrived a plan to get rid of him. "Here
comes the dreamer," one of them said. "Let's throw him in the
pit until we can decide what to do with him."

Later that day, a band of traders from Midian came by and
Joseph's brothers sold him to them. The Midianites brought
Joseph to Egypt and sold him to Potiphar, an Egyptian officer
and captain of the bodyguard of Pharaoh. Over time, Joseph
excelled in Potiphar's house, and Potiphar saw how all that
Joseph touched prospered. Seeing this, Potiphar made Joseph
overseer over his home and put him in charge of everything
he possessed. Joseph was now second in command in Potiphar's house.

Joseph was a very handsome young man and caught the eye
of Potiphar's wife. She tried to seduce him one day, but Joseph
resisted her because of his loyalty to Potiphar. Embarrassed
by what she had done and Joseph's refusal to sleep with her,
she lied and said that Joseph had tried to molest her. Enraged
at this, Potiphar had Joseph thrown in prison.

While in prison, Joseph gained the respect of the chief jailer. The jailer was so impressed with Joseph's excellent spirit and abilities that he put Joseph in charge of all the prisoners. Joseph was responsible for whatever was done in the prison.

Joseph met the king's baker and cupbearer during that time, both of whom had offended Pharaoh. One night, the cupbearer and the baker each had a dream and were deeply troubled. They told Joseph their dreams, and he interpreted them. Then he said, "When you are delivered up to Pharaoh and my interpretations are correct, please remember to tell him who interpreted your dreams."

It came to pass for the baker and the cupbearer just as Joseph had said it would. The baker was executed and the cupbearer restored to the king's service. However, the cupbearer forgot to mention Joseph to Pharaoh.

Some time later, while Joseph was still in prison, Pharaoh himself had a dream. He called all his magicians and wise men to interpret the dream, but they could not. Then the cupbearer remembered Joseph and told Pharaoh what had happened in the prison.

Pharaoh summoned Joseph and told him about his dream and asked if Joseph could interpret it. Joseph did interpret the dream. He told Pharaoh of good harvests and famine and how to prepare. Pharaoh was so impressed with Joseph that he said, "Can we find a man like this, in whom is a divine spirit? . . . Since God has informed you of this, there is no one so discerning and wise as you are. You shall be over my house, and according to your command all my people shall do homage; only in the throne I will be greater than you" (Genesis 41:38–40).

With that, Joseph was made ruler over Egypt, with all authority and power—and made to ride in the second chariot.

At the end of Joseph's story, we find that a great famine has struck the land, even where his father, Jacob, and his brothers live. It happened that Joseph's family came to Egypt to buy food and had to buy it from Joseph. Recognizing his brothers,

Joseph concealed his identity until such a time that he could make sure that every member of his family could come to Egypt to escape the famine. When Joseph finally revealed his identity, his brothers feared retribution, but Joseph forgave them and they all found favor with Pharaoh.

It was through this series of events that all of Joseph's dreams were realized. Their sheaves bowed down to his sheaf, and the sun and the moon and eleven stars all bowed down to him. The dreams of faithful people do come true.

PART I

THE SUCCESSFUL
SUBORDINATE LEADER

1

Second and Successful

Second place does not mean second class.

WE CAN LEARN several things from Joseph's story.
Joseph was never the primary leader, but he was able
to save all of Egypt and Israel—even from the second chariot, a subordinate position. Dreams are not only for primary
leaders; subordinate leaders dream, too. So keep dreaming,
regardless of your circumstances or the people with whom
you work. When people do bad things to hurt you, handle
it rightly and it will turn out to your good. Just be faithful
everywhere you serve, whether in the prison or the palace.
Good deeds will somehow, someday be remembered. Just
when you need help with a project or the bosses support an
idea you have, the good deed will pay off.

Don't be afraid to show your strengths and abilities. They
may be just exactly what the king, or your boss, is looking for.
If you serve with excellence and integrity, you will be greatly

rewarded. If you have been mistreated and get the opportunity to retaliate, don't do it. Forgive instead. All that you lost will be restored.

Let's look at my definition of a subordinate leader; this definition fits anyone who is not in the number one position in his or her organization.

> The *subordinate leader* is not the first, not the primary, but is the minor, junior; he is not the dominant person in the organization.

As the "not dominant" second-position person, how does one reach his or her goals and fulfill their dream? For every subordinate leader the challenge remains to accomplish his dreams and live life to the fullest measure of success and happiness. It is my hope that this book will help you realize your potential by giving you insights that will encourage you and motivate you to be the kind of excellent second in command Joseph was. All things are possible in the future, no matter where you are seated right now.

Robert L. Webb, at www.motivation-tools.com, puts it like this: "A burning desire, with a bigger-than-life vision, can overcome all barriers."[1]

An individual's level of personal achievement is based on the size of their personal vision. Super-achievers have a vision that is bigger than life. Most people limit their goals to socially acceptable standards, instead of what they feel inside. Everyone has different talents, interests, and learning methods. Goals must be in harmony with these attributes. Finding harmony is another barrier to overcome. When harmony is found and a burning desire is established, success will be found no matter what your social surroundings or previous experience.

A burning desire is the foundation on which productive motivation is based. You do not need to hear motivational speakers or have money to start. You already have the start-up tool—creativity. Just use it. Dreams stimulate creative thinking. Turning dreams into mini-projects creates a burning desire, and many successful mini-projects are preparation for the bigger-than-life vision.

Every person, at some time in his life, desires to be an achiever. For many, this ambition has been destroyed. But under the right leadership, this latent desire can be brought back to life.

SUCCESS IN THE SECOND CHARIOT

Everyone is subordinate to someone—some board, some coach, some law, some other leader. To think that there is no hope of making a huge difference in this world from the number two position is to believe that only a lucky few will ever know significance. The truth is that significance has nothing to do with your position, but rather your service. As a matter of fact, serving is the only path to significance. If all a person does is live his life focused on his own selfish world and doesn't reach out to help others by serving them, he will live the most insignificant life there is.

Joseph had a dream that looked pretty egotistical from the outset. How it would all work out was beyond his control. The fact that he entered the arena of service first as a slave, then as a servant, and then as a prisoner ironically were the steps for the making of a champion. Joseph learned from suffering that true success and significance come from a humble and broken spirit. Just imagine being imprisoned for false charges during the prime of your life and then being forgotten by the only ones who could help you get out. Joseph must have had his days of discouragement and depression. He must have experienced anger and self-pity. But through all the trials, Joseph kept a spirit of excellence. Everything he put his hand to prospered.

So it is for anyone who has been dealt an unfair hand or raw deal; what you do with it will be your legacy. It is not what hand you are dealt that determines your destiny; it is how you play that hand. Turn misfortune into fortune, privilege into sacrifice and service, and you will make a difference.

SECOND AND SATISFIED

The founder of a global nonprofit organization was a man of many gifts and abilities. He was focused on the big picture and didn't pay much attention to those on the lower rungs of the organization. He had things to do and places to go, and he expected that his vice president, Stewart, would take care of the details. To land a private meeting with the founder was so difficult that Stewart had given up trying. He would wait to be called upon before he would ask for permission to give his ideas and opinions. Stewart was second in command, but there was quite a gap between him and first place.

Most of the other employees looked to Stewart for everything. He was the link between the top brass and the rank and file. Stewart was extremely capable in his own right and could easily lead the organization. He had the trust of the rest of the employees, the control of daily operations, and the network with every principle player in their field of operations. The position he was in perfectly fit his gift mix, and he soared relationally with nearly everyone in the organization.

Several people told Stewart that he should start his own thing or ask the founder to let him take the CEO spot. He was capable and more than qualified. But Stewart knew that first place might rob him of the opportunity to use his gifts in the same effective way he was used to, so he decided to stay in the second-place role and serve the founder and everyone else the way he was doing it. He was second and satisfied.

DICK CHENEY—THE MOST POWERFUL VICE PRESIDENT IN HISTORY

In an article in *USA Today*, Dick Cheney, vice president to George W. Bush, is viewed as the most powerful vice president in history. His power hasn't come from positioning himself to make a bid for president when George Bush's tenure is up, but because, as *USA Today* put it, "He is able to command unprecedented power because he has abandoned his ambition."[1]

In a climate where most vice presidents would be "in training" to take a run at the nation's top job, Dick Cheney has declared "non-intent" for the purpose of focusing on the success of his boss. "Cheney has told President Bush, their staffs and members of Congress that he won't run for president when Bush's tenure in the White House ends." As a result, Cheney has become the go-to guy on everything from making key appointments to defense policy to congressional relations.

Cheney's commitment not to run for president establishes his loyalty to the president and removes the sense of rivalry between him and congressional leaders. His motives aren't in question because he isn't trying to get special attention or publicity or gain political clout for personal reasons. He is simply a "second chariot" focused on the success of the "first chariot."

Cheney says, "Really, the key is that I'm available to do what he has to have done, and that I'm able to offer advice to him privately that doesn't show up in the newspapers. He knows that my only desire is to help him succeed, and that I will give it to him straight. He can be confident I will tell him exactly what I think."[2]

The power in this kind of relationship, between the first and second chariots, exists best in the absence of competition, the opportunity for honesty, and the abandonment of self-serving ambition for the sake of your leader's success. This is not a "best buddy" relationship, but one built upon mutual respect.

2

Dreams Are Always Possible, Regardless of Who Is Dreaming

Whether you think you can or whether you think you can't, you're right.[3]

—HENRY FORD

IT DOESN'T MATTER if it is the dream of the primary leader or the administrative assistant—it's still a dream. No one has the right to discredit your dream, much less steal it from you. If you have a dream, it's yours to keep—never give up on your dream.

Only if Joseph had forgotten and given up on his dream could he have been defeated in his mind and emotions. I can see him rehearsing the dreams over and over in the prison cell night after night. "I wonder how the sun, moon, and the eleven stars will bow down to me. What does that mean?" Then he would go on with his life. Later, he would find himself in the luxury of the king's palace and wonder, "What did it mean that the sheaves of my brothers would bow to my sheaf?" With all that he had to do for Potiphar, the jailer, and Pharaoh, he must have mulled those thoughts over and over again in his mind. It wouldn't be revealed to him what the dreams meant until he recognized his brothers when they appeared before him to buy food that momentous day in the storehouse of the king.

ANYONE WHO DREAMS WILL HAVE OPPONENTS

To dream is to go outside the norm, to look beyond the obvious, and to ignore limitations set by those around you. It is to tempt others to reject and oppose, but we must dream nevertheless. Joseph's brothers and Potiphar's wife could do nothing but become an integral part of the predetermined plan. Angry and full of hate, they were part of what eventually made Joseph great. Their actions put Joseph in the place where he met the king's servants and eventually got an audience with him. So it is with those who oppose your dream—they are tools in the divine hand to make your dream possible.

People don't understand your dreams, especially when your dreams bring you outside of their control or self-imposed restrictions. Most people reject those who want to better their situation if it means breaking out of the circle of their limitations. "You can't do that!" "You're crazy! Nobody would buy into that!" They respond this way because they have no dreams of their own. You will encounter resistance, but you must follow your dream.

Then there are those insecure leaders who feel threatened by the *scale* of your dreams. Someone in the organization will always put a "you better watch him or her" in the boss's ear. All this serves to do is put the relationship off balance and waste precious time until the boss can trust you again.

It's hard to understand everyone's dreams. Dreams bring your imagination into virtual reality, a place where you can live out the possibilities of where you want to go and who you want to be. When people share their dreams with me of a new business or new church or some great idea, it is my job to dream with them, to try to see it the way they do, and, if possible, to buy into that dream. When I do that, I have the chance to make that dream a reality—for them.

SERVE THE SERVANTS...
SERVE THE KING...JUST SERVE

There is something divine about serving. Christ did it with incredible humility and made it the most regal act toward mankind. He gave it a sense of worth as no one else could have. We should serve with humility and pure motives, because our service carries the same value and virtue whether it is done for the lowliest servant or the highest royalty. The characteristics are the same: humility, selflessness, and honor to the one you serve. Joseph served in excellence and found the favor he needed to be the deliverer his destiny had determined he would be. He was totally committed to making the king successful—which would be Joseph's success.

We sometimes find ourselves sitting next to great leaders in boardrooms, sharing luxurious meals with the wealthy, or participating in a benefit for the less fortunate. In every case, there they are—the servants, making us comfortable, making us feel important. But they are also important. We must realize that any privilege, any advantage afforded us, is ours only to share with others, not to keep. We must share with knave and nobility alike by serving with whatever is put in our hands to give and to do.

GOOD DEEDS ARE GOOD SEEDS

"I have found the paradox. If you love until it hurts, then there can be no more hurt, only more love." No one in modern history has done more good deeds or sown more hope and love than Mother Teresa. I have had the opportunity to serve with hundreds of leaders and ministers from around the world. Many are godly and great in their gifting, but none matched the level of selflessness and self-sacrifice on behalf of the needy exhibited by Mother Teresa. When asked at a meeting of leaders who was the most admired person in the world out of Michael Jordan, Ronald Reagan, Abraham Lincoln, Bill Gates, Julia Roberts, or Mother Teresa, 100 percent responded, "Mother Teresa." Was it her doctrine? Was it her creed? Was it just love? Or was it the need? Need is often the greatest motivator of successful people.

Of all the great leaders in her time, few had the moral stature, influence, or respect this tiny missionary to the starving and hurting of India had. She will be remembered as being a greater person than most of our presidents, all of our CEOs, and our sports superstars, yet all she wanted was to do good deeds for those who needed help. The seeds she has sown have created awareness for hurting people, and her life has given us the example to follow to meet the needs of others.

Joseph's service to the baker and the cupbearer was the seed that grew into his ascent to the palace. In the palace he was able to carry out the ultimate good deed of rescuing the land and its inhabitants from starvation due to an impending famine.

You must look for opportunities to do good deeds for those around you. It may start out subtly but then become more obvious. Sowing seeds of kindness and consideration for others will bring a great harvest of cooperation later. Random acts of kindness will reap the same toward you someday. Someday, when you need it the most, your good deeds will be remembered.

DISPLAY YOUR GIFTS TO THE KING; HE JUST MIGHT USE THEM

Nothing offered boastfully is received gracefully. Joseph never offered his knowledge and understanding as a means to get control or get in the limelight. His knowledge was displayed so that it would be applied toward fulfillment of the dream. The king said, "Can we find a man like this, in whom is a divine spirit?...There is no one so discerning and wise as you are"

(Gen. 41:38–39). Joseph wasn't flaunting, but he also wasn't hiding the fact that he had the goods.

Someone said, "I offer my gifts anywhere they can be used to meet a need." In many cases your abilities and talents are exactly what the doctor ordered. In these times it is no virtue to hide them or pretend that you don't have them. Put them on the table for everyone to see, and use them for the benefit of the enterprise. This is not boasting; it is utilization of the gifts you possess.

MAKE YOUR GREATEST STRENGTHS EXCELLENCE AND INTEGRITY

When you are honest with yourself and others, it will radiate in an almost subconscious way. Integrity is hard to read, but it is easily felt. Either you carry it with you like the shirt on your back, or you come across as someone who might not be trustworthy. Joseph's excellent spirit was perceived by the king as a "spirit of the divine." Don't you know that from that point on, Joseph didn't have to deal with a credibility gap? Something about his excellent manner, confidence, and self-assured attitude gave him favor with the king.

And these kings were skeptics—they had cupbearers who would drink from their glass of wine to test it to see if it was poisonous. If it was poisonous, the cupbearer died. The king would get another cupbearer and another glass of wine. People died just because of his cautious nature, yet he empowered Joseph with the leadership of his empire because Joseph interpreted a dream. It was more than Joseph's discerning of dreams that landed him the position. It was his excellent spirit and radiating integrity.

TRY FORGIVENESS INSTEAD OF RETALIATION

It goes without saying that after Joseph's brothers sold him into slavery at the young age of seventeen and he spent his best years in slavery and in prison, Joseph had an axe to grind.

Most of us would have lain awake at night thinking of all the things we were going to do to the brothers if we ever got the chance. Well, Joseph got the chance. He had them right where he wanted them. He could have executed them or had them put in prison—but he forgave. Once he had them cornered, he let them out. With this one stroke of forgiveness, Joseph made amends for all his bad reports about his brothers to their father and his ostentatious dreams, and for their hatred and attack on him. This act of forgiveness brought peace and healing to his father's house.

It is almost *never* good to retaliate. Once an offense is committed against you, forgive. Let the powers that be settle the score. You may remove yourself from the situation that brought on the offense, but to scheme and plan some way to retaliate is more devastating to you than to the offender, for you will have to pay for any act you commit against him or her.

In your company or office, you cannot create camaraderie and unity with an attitude of always trying to settle the score with someone who has offended you. Payback is a given for every evil and underhanded deed, but it doesn't have to come from you.

3

Shifting Your Thinking

We are not in a position in which we have nothing to
work with. We already have the capacities, talents, directions, missions, callings.[4]

—ABRAHAM MASLOW

To PROGRESS IN this world, in your company, in your calling, in your work, leave a trail of successes everywhere
you go. Make your mark before you make your mark. Like
Joseph, you must leave a positive mark everywhere you serve.
These marks become the road map of your success. Reflecting
on each mark will give you insights into the next position you
hold. Eventually you will reach your life goal and make a huge
impact on some enterprise, some individual, some cause. Here
are some examples of people who made their mark before they
made their mark.

Lee Iacocca

Lido A. Iacocca was born on October 15, 1924. (Lido changed
his name to Lee after going to work for Ford. He felt it would
be easier for business associates and contacts to recognize and
understand.) Lee was never afraid of work. When he was ten

years old, he would take his wagon to the grocery store and wait outside. As shoppers came out, he would offer to pull their groceries home for a tip. When he turned sixteen, he worked sixteen hours a day in a fruit market. Lee attributes his work ethic to the example set by his father.

Lee went to Lehigh University. After graduating from Lehigh, he landed a job with Ford but put it on hold because he won the Wallace Memorial Fellowship at Princeton. He graduated from Princeton and started working for Ford in 1946.

Lee undertook the Fairlane Committee project. This committee used research data to decide what type of new car to produce. The car needed to be small, but also capable of holding four passengers. There would be a 2,500-pound limit, and the cost could not exceed $2,500, with equipment. It also needed to appeal to several markets at once. The consumer needed to feel comfortable driving the car to church, to the drag strip, or to the country club. The ultimate goal was to develop one basic car with a wide range of options so the customer could buy as much economy or luxury as he could afford. The end product was the 1964 Mustang.

This project allows us a glimpse at Lee's business management style. He used good marketing research data, he surrounded himself with good people, and he was willing to listen. He was also willing to take the risk of introducing a new product. All of this combined to make the Mustang a success. Lee became known as the father of the Mustang. Iacocca made his mark as a subordinate by producing the Mustang before he went to Chrysler, where he became a world-famous icon for leadership.

After the huge success of the Mustang, Lee was made president of Ford on December 10, 1970. He quickly realized that his job as president was far different from that of a manager. He now had to cut costs and increase profits instead of selling, marketing, and designing. By the end of 1975, Lee began having trouble at Ford. Most of it seemed to be a personality conflict between Henry Ford II and Lee. The tension continued to escalate, and Lee was fired in July 1978. But he didn't sit around for long. He joined forces with Chrysler on November 2, 1978.

It didn't take long for Lee to figure out that Chrysler was in a state of emergency. There was a serious lack of communication and no teamwork. He had to go to the government for government-backed loans. He also bargained with the union for cuts in salary and benefits. He reduced his salary to one dollar per year to show that everyone at the company must be willing to sacrifice if Chrysler was to survive. By 1983, Lee had Chrysler back on its feet, and on July 13, 1983, Chrysler paid back all the government loans. Lee made a public statement: "We at Chrysler borrow money the old-fashioned way. We pay it back."

Iacocca made his mark as a manager, in a subordinate role, before he became the president and primary leader of Ford and eventually Chrysler.[5]

Arnold Schwarzenegger

Arnold Schwarzenegger is a modern-day example of how to make your mark before you realize your greatest dreams.

Arnold Schwarzenegger was a skinny teenager living in Austria when, despite his parents' doubts, he threw himself into weight lifting. He went to the local gym three times a week, and each evening he worked out at home for several hours. Today, the champion bodybuilder turned actor is the biggest box office draw in the history of movies—to a great extent because of his physique. Now, of course, Arnold Schwarzenegger is governor of California. He never lost his dream.

Condoleeza Rice

Small beginnings do not mean impossible dreams. When Condoleeza Rice, national security adviser to President George W. Bush, was in high school, she was told that her test scores showed she probably wouldn't do well in college. Rice didn't take that to heart. Instead, she modeled herself after her grandfathers—one of whom had worked three jobs to support his family and the other who had completed college in 1920. She dedicated herself to her studies with such concentrated energy that she entered the University of Denver at age fifteen and graduated Phi Beta Kappa, the oldest and largest honor society in the nation, at nineteen. At age forty-one, Rice became the youngest provost in the history of Stanford University, the first woman and the first African-American to fill that prestigious post.

CHANGING POINT OF VIEW

In the mid-seventies, a small group of people started a new church in West Monroe, Louisiana, and I was the pastor. This small beginning turned out to be an incredible journey, one from which we would learn many lessons. Even though, as a family, we would encounter many difficult times associated with starting and leading a new church in a town we weren't from, we learned lessons about the value of staying true to the call on one's life and to each other.

For my family, the work was difficult at first, but after a while we began to see positive results. People were coming, the congregation was growing, and we were all learning how to effectively serve and lead others. It seemed that it wouldn't be very long before we would be ready to move to bigger and better things. But, as if God was trying to make us realize the importance of patient learning, we felt impressed that promotion would not come for many years. The impression was correct. Ten years passed before we began to experience the acceptance and respect of our peers as a leader in their world.

After leading this small church for seven years, my family moved to Germany to start a publishing company that would distribute counseling booklets and evangelism materials to German-speaking Europe. This was another great learning experience for us. We spent three years gaining the acceptance of those with whom we worked, those who would benefit from the information in these booklets, and our service to them. After that, we spent more years working alongside and building strong relationships with people that we still respect and consider friends today.

STEPPING UP FROM FIRST TO SECOND

When our family returned to the United States, we started two more churches. Then we moved to Baton Rouge, Louisiana, where I took a position as an assistant pastor with a large, growing church there. This was the first time in nearly fifteen years that I was serving in a subordinate position. Having been the primary leader in everything I was involved in during the last fifteen years, it would be a challenge to take the backseat. When hired, I was "junior" to ten other men on staff. As the learning process began, many difficult times came as well. But the value of what was learned is still shaping my life today.

It was interesting to watch each of my peers and how they approached their position of responsibility. Some had great vision for what they wanted their life to become. Others just followed orders, taking up new tasks as they were assigned, dropping previous ones as the direction from the top changed. Some worked as apprentices, as if they were training for some great future responsibility. Others had no dream except to make it through the next staff meeting without being dressed down for their failure to reach last month's goals. There was a clear distinction between those who dreamed and those who didn't. How my attitude would be affected by serving with other subordinates would help me realize the importance of this level of leaders.

Within a couple of years, I was asked to assume the senior associate pastor role, a position that posed new challenges for me. The focus in this position was not on how successful I could be, or on just getting the position, but about how to make the staff better and more effective at what they do. Ultimately, my goal was to make my boss as successful as possible. My position wasn't the real reward; it was the new opportunity.

Though difficult to avoid, being position-oriented is a downfall for many people. The goal should be to find the most effective way to serve in the organization. You can do this by encouraging each person in the organization and providing leadership in subtle ways. Roll up your sleeves and pitch in whenever you can to make each person successful. However, I had to learn how to lead from a lower level of leadership. As the position of second in command fleshed itself out, I learned key strategies that would help me to lead more consistently.

One strategy that is useful in leading from a subordinate position is to produce a written document that can be used to provide clarity and direction. This document then becomes the "starting point" on which most future decisions are based. The most significant thing, however, is to recruit workers—get other people in the organization involved in the process. Then establish training goals for those who need to be involved. If you multiply your skills in others who are part of a team, you will accomplish more and gain influence with your superiors.

Friends told me that it would be difficult for me to work for anyone else because I had been the primary leader in other organizations, which would make it hard to give up that sense of control. It would be a challenge, but working in a large, influential ministry as a subordinate was bigger than what I was doing alone. Becoming a strong leader is sometimes facilitated by first learning how to follow. It was a struggle for me for a long time.

Success in the second or third position has to be defined differently than when you are in the first position. The bottom-line measurements of success, which reveal the primary leader's accomplishments, almost never reflect directly on what you do from the second-in-command spot. Their desire to have success, however, is just as real regardless of the position you hold. Learning the importance of working as a subordinate is necessary to understanding how to define success in that position. Learning the skills to be successful as a subordinate leader takes time. But to make your mark, it is vital to learn the keys that help you accomplish the goals of your superiors. Every lesson learned adds to your treasure chest of knowledge and skill, which help establish your leadership and influence in the organization.

One way to make your mark is to be sure to faithfully accomplish one specific task to the delight of those you work for. Recruit a team to work with you to ensure that you accomplish the task successfully. Then take advantage of the wisdom and experience of those around you. Use your own brain, but also brainstorm with others to come up with creative ideas that make a plan better and more successful. When you succeed, give the credit to those who helped you. Then do it again and involve others, using their creative ideas to improve on what your team has done. Celebrate your success with the team. When you have a great product, training course, or idea, take it to those who would benefit from it. Get their buy-in and repeat it, making it better in the process. Remember to share the success with everyone involved in the win. Then go on to the next project and follow the same scenario.

Your superiors like to see success from their team no matter how far down the organizational chart they have to look. When a subordinate way down on level five begins to display brilliance and creativity, and the second- and third-level members aren't, chances are that the fifth-level employee will soon find him- or herself in the upper levels of the organization.

Remember, the bottom line is success and profit, growth and quality, and whoever produces it gets the credit and the promotion. With the promotion comes the acclaim and recognition that puts you in the spotlight to be awarded the next important task or assignment. As you continue to perform with excellence, your personal stock goes up, you get more of the best assignments, and the process begins to replicate itself. You cannot progress off of someone else's record of success; you must have your own. Look at what Abraham Lincoln said: "Always bear in mind that your own resolution to succeed is more important than any other thing."[6]

As I grew in the role of subordinate leader, I begin to think that this position had great potential. It was not just a holding pattern for my abilities, but rather it was a place where I could exercise my gifts and abilities and realize success.

THE DREAM POSITION

Another key to raising your personal stock and your position in an organization is to identify the "dream" position you want. This is the position that someone else may possess at the moment but you know you were cut out for. Once you have identified it, study it, find ways to improve, make suggestions, and then volunteer to work alongside the person to make him or her more successful. This is a commitment "to do the job before you get the job." Be available to share the tasks with the one who holds the place you want, and learn to do those tasks as well as or better than him. This positions you for that spot when he is promoted. Instead of using political means of undermining your superior, work to make him or her successful. If you are the person most responsible for them advancing, it is likely that you will fill their position. But remember, you must develop your own successor before you can move up the ladder. With no one to fill your position, you are stuck there.

These ideas for success in the subordinate position are the roads less traveled in organizations today. But realize that there is really no competition for the greater opportunities that are in your organization or in your life. You see, you create those opportunities.

For me, after a few years of working hard and leading from the second-place spot, opportunity to start living my dream came to me. It did not include getting promoted in the organization; it came from increased outside influence because of being part of a successfully growing organization.

As our church began to grow in its small-group ministry, it influenced hundreds and eventually thousands of other pastors and church leaders from around the world who came to see how we were doing it. As the coordinator of the small-group ministry, I had visibility and the attention of all who came. This opened doors of opportunity all over the world to teach and train churches and the leaders of these churches. It soon led to a book deal, which led to more success and exposure in my field. *The Cell-Driven Church* has been published in several languages and is used as a textbook for small-group ministry in several countries and the United States today. Though not exactly as notable as saving an entire nation from starvation, as Joseph did, it was a measure of success for me beyond my personal expectations. All of this transpired while serving as second in command.

THE SECOND-IN-COMMAND CULTURE

Four cultures exist in most organizations—more in some, less in others—but these four are almost always present:

1. *The Primary Leader(s)*—chief and principal leaders

2. *The Subordinate Leaders*—second in command and other leaders

3. *The Support Staff*—administrative and personal assistants

4. *The Implementers*—those who carry out the service or sales

Just as CEOs and corporate presidents enjoy a top-level culture, those in the second position, the support staff, and the implementers enjoy their own unique culture. Each cultural level within an organization has its own challenges as well as privileges and recognition. I have watched senior leaders of organizations huddle and talk about the "high things" to the exclusion of all others not so honored. But at the same time, I noticed how these top leaders go to each other to share their problems and struggles. They need this support system with others that face the same challenges and experience the same struggles. It is a good thing.

Just as our primary leaders interact with each other, we who are in the second chariot have our own circle of friends and leaders that we huddle with. We have our own set of challenges, our own peculiar issues that rock our world. It is a club, an unheralded society that only those in subordinate roles understand. We need each other and support each other. We know that without us, number one would not be the success that he or she is today. But we are satisfied to dream their dreams with them, setting our dreams aside and working toward their fulfillment. Therefore we support and proclaim the greatness of our leaders and enjoy the rewards that fall from their tables to us, their servants below.

The Need to Discern the Second-Place Culture

Second chariot leaders have great opportunities before them. Is it possible that we in the second-place position don't discern the opportunities available to us? We are so focused on trying to be number one, or at least trying to change number one, that we lose sight of the importance of our place in the enterprise. If we would pull the subordinate staff together and work as a united team, we would be able to accomplish more and also be a much greater benefit to the boss and ultimately the company.

Realize how important you are to the success of your firm, and rally others to do the same. You can make a great difference! This is also true of support staff. What a difference they make, and what a greater difference they could make by understanding their worth and the value of a highly developed support staff culture. The support staff must understand their culture as much as those in other subordinate leadership roles.

THE IMPORTANCE OF LOWER LEVEL LEADERS

No organization can grow and make a real impact in their field without strong leaders in every level of the organization. The leader at the top can't provide leadership at every level; others need to provide that leadership. Look at seven ways lower level leaders add to the primary leader's strength.

1. *Connecting*—these leaders provide connection between others in the organization, making everyone in the organization "visible."

2. *Continuity*—lower level leaders are the "vision conduit" that carries the vision down to others in the organization.

3. *Consistency*—transferring information in a consistent and timely manner is the task of middle managers and leaders.

4. *Congruency*—these leaders create a natural flow of information and motivation to the completion of every project.

5. *Confidence*—they provide the primary leader the confidence that every base is covered and that a predictable outcome can be expected.

6. *Correction*—through lines of accountability, progress and quality are maintained and slight corrections are administered.

7. *Completion*—leaders in the middle insure completion of goals through constant problem solving and adjustment till the job is done.

The need for leaders at many different levels is paramount to the success of any organization. Develop these leaders, and you will have more success.

I'M QUALIFIED TO DO THIS JOB, SO MOVE OVER

In the mind of David Huntsfield, he was the most qualified person in the company to take the leadership role, and everyone else should follow. After all, he earned his MBA at Vanderbilt, was the top in his class, and didn't need anyone telling him what to do. No one in the company could come near him in intelligence and leadership ability. So move over, here comes David!

David had a strong-willed mother, and his father was a self-made millionaire who always seemed to question David's ability to succeed in life. His mother was mainly interested in what she wanted out of life and would only become amused if David did something noteworthy, something that no one else could do. He had a lot to prove, and he wasn't going to let anyone get in his way.

The boss was weak in many areas of his leadership, and though very much a steady producer, he could not bring the company into the place where it needed to be. David had to come up with a plan where he could outshine the boss, grab the limelight, and get the number-one position in the company. It's what he had worked for all those years in college, and he wasn't going to let this lackluster personality that everyone called "boss" get in his way.

His plan was to discover every weakness the boss had, record every mistake he made, and make sure the board of directors found out about it in a discreet way. David knew that if he could show the board where the boss was missing it, they would give him the job and fire the boss. Nothing was going to stop him on his way to the top.

NO-MAN'S-LAND

When you find yourself dreaming of how it would be to run the company and sit in the head office, make sure you don't end up in "no-man's-land." No-man's-land is that place of discontent where your desire to be number one has caused you to lose influence with your peers. You are looking up and therefore do not see those around you. You overlook those in your own culture and fail to meet their expectations of you. In this dilemma, you are no good to your level of peers and are a threat to, or at least in competition with, the primary leader. You are in no-man's-land. This is the quickest way out of an organization. If David's plan is discovered, he will be out in no-man's-land.

Everyone wants to be the primary leader because of the accolades that seem to flow toward them. Being in the front means you get noticed and get the credit when things go well. You have the first choice of office, furniture, travel, and perks, which gives you the sense of importance, power, and control. This is normal in all of us, but unchecked, as in David's case, it can lead to disaster in an organization.

THE DEAD END

Every business, church, industry, and organization has a culture that exists before you get there. These cultures are close-knit and sometimes very hard to break into. You should realize that the day when you are accepted in that culture may never come. This is especially true of family businesses or organizations where ownership of the vision is closely held by a few individuals near the top.

What makes this environment a "dead end" is the fact that until you are accepted into the culture of the organization, you will never be able to exercise your gifts to their fullest potential—no matter how desperately your gifts are needed in the organization.

For example, if your gift is leadership, but the "owners of the vision" feel threatened by that gift, you may never be allowed an opportunity to lead without their control. Every attempt to lead or bring in fresh ideas will be thwarted behind closed doors by those closest to the boss.

To get into a tightly held culture, you may have to learn how to maneuver within it. You should be faithful in the little things you are given to do until you have proven your loyalty and are no longer a threat to those who are in control. To get in, you will have to be invited! If you are never invited in, consider whether this is where you want to stay. Therefore, know where you fit into the big picture and develop an appreciation for that place. While serving faithfully in that position you will have the opportunity to develop strong relationships with key people. Your patience will provide you with a big payoff sooner or later.

FIND YOUR SUCCESS LEVEL

Another way to break into an organization's culture is to find the place in the organization where you are not a threat and can still function in your gifting. In other words, if you are resisted as vice president of the corporation, move down to assistant vice president, division head, or even lower—until you find the place where you can operate in your gift freely. When you have done this and successfully performed unobstructed, you will be recognized by those at every level and then moved up as trust levels increase. This is the "bloom where you are planted" scenario. It may take time but could be worth the wait.

FIND YOUR CULTURE AND SERVE THERE

Learn to be faithful to your own business or relational culture at the level where you presently function, and be great there. If you cannot be great at the cultural level where you are now, you may not be great at the next level. Mother Teresa worked in the culture of the poverty-stricken and diseased, became a champion of their cause, and won the admiration of every great leader in the world. Discern the challenges and needs at your level, and become a champion within that culture. This will serve as the practice you need to be great when you are promoted.

Successful leaders of nations serve their cultures, CEOs and company presidents serve their cultures, and we need to serve our own culture. When a leader fails to serve his culture, he ends up exploiting that culture, as in Iraq and recently in Haiti. This is an example of exploiting those in a culture and having the people turn against you in hate and revolt. It is essential to understand and believe that we can help make people's dreams come true. We also add to the success of those that we follow. All the while, we know that our day, our dream, will come—maybe without fanfare, maybe silently, maybe secretly, but come it will.

THE NETWORK

People are your connections for success over the long haul. So learn to network with others at the second level. When dealing with successful people, realize that time is their greatest resource and that they can't just give their time to everyone who wants a private conversation. Leaders should spend their hours networking with other primary leaders to have maximum influence and impact with their peers. This is why they have personal assistants and administrative assistants. John Maxwell, *New York Times* best-selling author of *The 21 Irrefutable Laws of Leadership*, is one of those highly successful people whose time is parceled out very carefully to get the maximum productivity from every minute he is awake. It is unlikely that he would spend his time trying to network with the second-in-command leader in your business. John networks with other primary leaders in the business world in order to influence as many of them as possible. He is gracious and will speak to you at a conference he might be giving, but he networks with top leaders.

Now, it is very difficult to get John Maxwell on the phone to ask if he's available to hold a leadership seminar or speak at a fund-raiser for your organization. However, organizations that I have worked for have been able to secure his services by working through his "second in command" on several occasions, and he brought value and credibility to what was being done. It is your responsibility as second in command to network with other seconds in command in order to secure the services of their primary leaders. The way you do this is to *make friends with the second in command* in the organizations with which you want to form strategic alliances. You may also want to connect with their administrative and personal assistants. These are the people in close proximity to number-one leaders.

Because subordinate leaders, especially second-in-command leaders, have their own culture, you need to understand it and learn how to work within it to build relationships and long-term friendships. Learn what their goals are and help them reach them. Understand that the subordinates of any primary leader have goals they need to reach on behalf of their leader. Therefore, make sure that what you are asking them to do, which involves their time and perhaps the time of their leader, helps them to complete their goals. Chances are they are not going to stop what they are doing to help you accomplish some unrelated goal of yours.

It is also helpful to know what will make your idea a win for everyone involved. If you miss the fact that someone in the organization might not think your idea is a win for him personally, he can shoot it down in the staff meeting when it is presented. Find out what makes it a win for the decision makers, and present the win-win proposition. Then *network with their vision.* It is not enough to buy into their product or service, but you should also buy into their vision. When you get excited about what the other organization is doing and promote it, then they view you as a strong proponent and a partner.

EQUIP is a nonprofit organization whose vision is to train one million Christian leaders around the world in six years. It is called the *Million Leaders Mandate.* Frankly, that is exciting and worthy of promotion everywhere I go. Promoting the *Million Leaders Mandate* extensively has afforded me the opportunity to represent EQUIP as the European coordinator. What a great privilege. Networking with their vision and becoming an integral part to help them see it accomplished is a great honor. As a result, I have been given the chance to do something with them greater than I ever would have had the opportunity to do on my own.

Leverage the influence.

When you are able to connect and partner with great leaders and their causes, you gain influence from them that helps you fulfill greater goals than ever before. With the influence you get from other great leaders, you can influence many others to work with you, through networks, to accomplish great things. By using the influence your leader and the leaders you network with have in the marketplace, you are in a relational position to gain the cooperation of other leaders. It is my conviction that you should do everything in your power to leverage the influence of the organization you work for and the influence of your leader. This promotes what they are doing, and in return you get…*influence.*

Second in command has influence with the boss.

More than anyone else, because of proximity and relationship, the second in command is usually the one with the most influence with the boss in company affairs. Exceptions to that are family, personal assistants, and executive assistants. In that case, remember that with all great leaders, there is someone in whom they confide and trust. Find out who that person is, and build a strong mutual trust relationship.

As you shift your thinking to realize how important the second-in-command position is to an organization, you will become more effective and productive in everything you do.

4

Understand Your Role

In every initiative and adventure, it is necessary to gain wisdom and understanding in order to have a successful journey. It is also true for the second in command to understand what is required to stay functional and effective in the organization.

—AUTHOR

As second in command in an organization, you must understand your role.

KNOW WHAT'S GOING ON AROUND YOU

Nothing is more embarrassing than to have something major take place in your organization—and you not know about it. When a subordinate is totally informed and you are totally blank, you feel that the information loop just passed you by. Stay informed! Sometimes the only way this can be accomplished is for you to stay in the trenches until the project is well on its way to success and maintain a strong reporting/ feedback system.

STAY PUT!

When you assume the number-two role, you should stay where the day-to-day action is. You can't manage what you can't see. My personal experience is that the enormous amount of travel I do disqualifies me for a number-two role. Even though you may thrive in that role under normal circumstances, unless you can stay close to the fire, it is inevitable that you will lose touch with day-to-day developments.

This actually occurred at the ministry I work at now. I was the executive pastor at Seacoast Church, but I still traveled a lot doing seminars and consultation for churches about small-group ministry. As the director of a church-planting organization that needed my time, and being in demand by several ministries located overseas, too much of my time was spent away from my work at home. Even working hard when in town was not enough to take up the slack caused by my being away when needed. My pastor and I discussed the situation, and the only realistic option was for me to take a position that allowed me to be gone from time to time and meant my presence would not needed on a week-to-week basis. It also meant that my position would not need to be highly informed. Proximity to the daily operations of the organization is a requirement that needs to be met in order to fulfill the second-in-command position.

YOU MAY NOT BE SUCCESSFUL
AS A NUMBER-ONE LEADER

Michael Gerber defines the term *e-myth* as "the fatal assumption that an individual who understands the technical work of a business can successfully run a business that does technical work."[7] It might help to add that it is also a fatal assumption to think that just because you have years of experience as a number-two leader, you can run an organization as number one. It is possible, but not necessarily so. Your gifts would determine that. If, of course, you have prepared for the lead role and feel you can do it, then go for it. But consider this: experience as a second in command is not the only experience you need. Your destiny may be CEO, and the skills you gain on the way up may qualify you for the job. However, ask yourself, "Am I really cut out for the lead position?" If you aren't, then be satisfied to be a great and successful number-two leader.

John Maxwell talks about the benefits of being a number two who works alongside a good number one in his Injoy Life Club tape "Second and Satisfied." With permission from John, here are some of his insights and stories.

BENEFITS OF BEING NUMBER TWO

> Following a good leader gives you an opportunity to work in a "success" environment.

> It also allows you to work in an environment of growth and development.

> You get the opportunity to be exposed to great leaders, people, and experiences.

> You get the opportunity to use your strengths.

> It affords you an atmosphere from which it is easier to lead others.

> The work is bigger than you can do alone; the opportunities are greater than you can create alone.

Note: Once you distinguish yourself in the organization, you are ready to take on more of the upper-level assignments and positions. Stay on the lookout for opportunities to add value to the organization and for projects to get involved in where you can use your skill and influence to make them more successful. When you have made your mark at the lower, perhaps entry, levels of the organization, you will have a much better chance of moving into positions at the upper levels. Other insights John shares include the advantage of being on a successful team.

GOOD NUMBER TWOS MAKE THEIR LEADERS MORE SUCCESSFUL

There is a story about one Chicago Bulls player being interviewed after Michael Jordan scored sixty-nine points in a winning effort. The interviewer asked the player, "What was the most rewarding thing you were able to be involved in playing with the Bulls?" The player responded, "It was the night Michael Jordan and I scored seventy points." He scored one point, and Michael Jordan scored sixty-nine. But it is the team score that counts at the end of the game.

Good number twos make up for the weaknesses of their leaders. They complement, accentuate, fill up, and add value to their leaders in every situation.

They bring addition and multiplication to their leaders' efforts. *Synergy* describes the benefits a good second in command brings to the leader. Together you can accomplish more than the sum total of what you can do separately. As a member of a team, you can share in the victories great leaders will bring to the team.

After years of faithful service, you may even get the chance to call the plays. It has been my experience that many number-one leaders appreciate it when their number-two person can take over responsibilities and lead the team to victory.

What makes the number-two position difficult is often caused by the environment we grow up in. For the most part, we live in an egotistical world that only looks out for... that's right, *number one*. Accepting the role as number two is accepting some inherent difficulties. Consider these.

As number two, your success is affected by the success or failure of the leader. You may actually do a great job, and yet the leader may fail. It's tough to sit back and let that happen, but it happens all the time. In situations like this you must remember to remain faithful to all those you serve. Understand that your career may not be limited to your present position, but you must serve like it is.

As number two, you are expected to put someone else's agenda above your own. You are brought on to assist the leader in making the enterprise successful. In that, you find success and flourish. If you try to use the enterprise to advance your stature or success, you will end up undermining the organization. So you put your agenda aside. Let your loyalty and performance make room for you in the future successes of life.

As number two, you put your ego in check and sometimes bench certain abilities and talents. We bring many gifts, talents, abilities, and training to the table when we come on board. The truth is that you will only use the abilities and gifts that benefit the enterprise and nothing else. So you sit on gifts and expertise that are not relevant to your position or that someone else is providing.

As number two, your momentum is canceled when the boss changes directions or procedures without notice. Your job description may change, too. Just as you begin to feel that you have it all together, your schedule finally worked out, and those you lead on a daily basis have bought into the new thrust…it all changes. Now the resell begins. Keeping the boss's decision in the best light, you begin the process of reselling the new ideas to a skeptical group of followers. This can be a difficult part of the number two's job. It is necessary to learn the skill of selling the new ideas that come from the front office.

How Do I Know Which Leader to Work For?

Let's face it, not every partnership or staff appointment is a match. With each enterprise there is a culture, and you must fit in or it will not work. There are a lot of great leaders that you just could not work for. They accomplish great things for their organization and do great things for their world, but they would not be a match for you. Sometimes it is not the leader but others on staff that spoil the match-up. So how do you know who is the right leader to work for? Here is some more wisdom from Dr. John C. Maxwell.

QUESTIONS THE NUMBER TWO SHOULD ASK ABOUT THE NUMBER ONE

> Do I respect number one? Does he or she respect me?

> Do I like being around him or her?

> Do I agree with the vision and purpose of the enterprise?

> Can I grow in this setting?

> Do I complement his or her gifts?

> Can I accomplish more under this person or by myself?

> Does this person believe in me?

> Does my leader support me?

> Will my leader mentor me and add value to my life?

> Does this leader have my best interest at heart?

In other words, will this be a one-way street where you do all the giving, make all the sacrifices, and take the rap for failures? Or will you be elevated, encouraged, and acknowledged for your contributions? It will only work if the number one values you as a person and will respect you and give you opportunities to be creative and find significance.

Leaders you don't want to work for are the controlling, insecure leaders that micro-manage every aspect of your life. It is also very difficult to thrive in an environment where the leader is incompetent and unable to lead the organization. It is not your job to fix this kind of leader; rather, it is your job to add value and use your leadership gift to try to help them lead.

5

Qualifications of the Second Chariot

The question "Who ought to be boss?" is like asking,
"Who ought to be the tenor in the quartet?" Obviously,
the man who can sing tenor.[8]

—HENRY FORD

THERE ARE QUALIFICATIONS for every job worth having. The second-in-command position, however, is very complicated because of the relationship you must have with the boss, your peers, and your subordinates. It requires a lot of decision-making prowess as well as relational skills. It is one of those kinds of jobs where everyone else has the luxury of having a bad day once in a while, but you may not.

In every organization, specific areas of knowledge are required as well as formal or informal training that prepares someone to take on the challenge of second in command. I have pored over hundreds of job descriptions, and they vary greatly. So here are some minimal qualifications that have little to do with specifics as far as expertise is concerned, but they are nonnegotiable attributes that a good number two should possess.

1. *Uniqueness*—there is only one of you. It is not your title that qualifies you to lead; it is your uniqueness. You have a one-of-a-kind personality mix, talent mix, and network of friends and associates that no one on earth has, and there are people who will follow you and no one else. So lead on.

   Peter F. Drucker, known as the most important management thinker of our time, has been a mentor to many people across this country and around the world. But his goal is not to make people more like Peter F. Drucker, but to make each unique individual all that he or she can be. Self-discovery is something that not many people attain in life. When we discover who God has made us to be and how to be that person for Him and for others in our life, we discover our qualifications to lead.

2. *Experience*—the only way to get experience is to get experience, and this too takes time. You can't shortcut the experience issue. Years of dealing with circumstances, situations, and a variety of people will add to your bank of knowledge and skill.

3. *Similar abilities as the first in command*—second in command is really a military term used to designate the person who would take over command in case the first in command was killed. The need for the same level of expertise as the first in command is seen most clearly in the relationship between a jet pilot and his copilot. The copilot must have sufficient flying hours, pass equally difficult proficiency exams, and be able to complete an assignment with equal effectiveness as the pilot. The same scenario is true in any enterprise. The second in command must have equal abilities to run the corporation in case he is given the responsibility.

4. *A proven track record*—of successfully building a

business, services company, division, or position of similar nature to the one you will assume in the second-in-command position.

5. *Find the greatness in you*—it is too easy to see our weaknesses and resign to a defeated attitude. However, there is greatness in each one of us that God wants to display for all to see. It is in your gift, in your experience, in your personal knowledge, and in your relationships. Greatness, in other words, equals living up to your potential. Never compare yourself to what others have done—it doesn't count for you. Do all that you have the potential to do, and you will find greatness.

6. *The ability to build*—most leaders can maintain, some can manage change, but it takes a strong leader to build and grow a company. A second in command must be able to build a complete and strong management team that gets the job done. You can't get in the way of management; you must lead the way.

7. *Excellent interpersonal skills*—number two should have the right personality. He will either be an asset to the boss or a constant source of discouragement and conflict if he does not possess the right communication skills. You should possess the ability to listen, relate, and communicate with a high level of integrity and regard for those with whom you work. This is the basis for cooperative relationships in the workplace.

8. *Creative, entrepreneurial*—the ability to troubleshoot problems, come up with creative solutions, start new departments, and expand existing ones with a high level of success are also important qualities to possess.

9. *Decisiveness*—you can't wait around for the boss to make all the decisions; this is what he hired you for.

It is the nature of your position. You will have to make dozens of decisions every week—so get ready.

10. *Patience*—someone asked me in a meeting the difference between faithfulness and patience. The answer is one that has helped me through the years: faithfulness is sticking it out with someone or some enterprise in all the ups and downs of life, accepting whatever circumstances come your way. Faithful people believe that their reward will come even after many trials and sacrifice. This is an incredible attribute to possess.

Patience, on the other hand, is waiting for the circumstances to work out in your favor. Many times in my life, impatience has cost me more than I wanted to pay. Impatience has caused me to act prematurely while circumstances were against me. Impatience can be blamed for many of our failures. Knowing when to act is equal to possessing the advantage and momentum.

Remember your parents saying, "Just be patient. When the ice cream man comes you will get a Popsicle"? Or, "Wait till you are sixteen, and you can get your driver's license"? A reward is always attached to patience. Patience for me is, "Giving God time to work things out in my favor." Whether with the boss, with the raise, or with some circumstance, patience brings many satisfying rewards to one's life.

PERSONAL TRAITS

You can never be someone else, but you can possess his or her traits. Find someone you admire and imitate him or her.

Loyalty—for me, making the success of the leader and the organization my success is a win for the boss *and* for me. Loyalty says to the boss and the entire organization, "I am here for the success of everyone involved, not just for me." This ends the rivalry and competition for position.

Flexibility—the ability to flow with change and take new directions without complaining is important if you are to stay useful and part of the team as it changes directions. Because change is inevitable for success in any organization, your ability to flex and bend and go along with change makes you a very valuable member.

Passionate—a lack of passion for accomplishment is a negative force in companies today. You should have a fervent desire for excellence and success for the enterprise. Be passionate about the goals and vision that your organization has and be a "player" in its success.

Confidentiality—it is inevitable, you will see the bad side of the leader because every leader has one. Make sure that no one else sees the boss's bad side through your eyes. What you learn about him or her, or what you hear him or her say to you in private or intense meetings with other staff should be a matter of strictest confidence. Do not reveal "classified information," information intended for a select part of the staff. Though it is a temptation to do so because you have privileged information that makes you feel important, the moment you leak that information, you cease to be important.

Committment—to date, I have been married thirty-seven years. It has been a remarkable journey together with my wife. We have seen many successes and many sorrows, many ups and lots of downs, and regardless of any conflict we have entered into, dedication to one another brought us through it all. Through thick and thin, we were committed to see the final win.

Humor—it is not enough to have backbone; you also need to have a funny bone. Being able to laugh is a great attribute in the stress and seriousness of a work environment.

Determination—be gritty. Have the resolve to see success regardless of the challenges you may face.

Dedication—this is enthusiastic devotion to the enterprise.

Trustworthy—be dependable. Build a reputation that you

can be trusted with facts and responsibility.

Stamina—untiring effort. Keep coming back after any set-backs until the victory is won.

LEADERSHIP SKILLS

Dr. John C. Maxwell says, "Everything rises and falls on leadership." In every organization there is someone leading, and the success of that organization will depend on that person's ability to lead. The following list of skills and character traits have been identified in many of the great leaders of our time.

Motivate—this is the ability to move others in the direction they need to go. It's having the capacity to cause people to take the initiative—to do what's right without being told to. Remember, knowing "why" we should do something motivates us more than knowing "how." Many people know how but they don't do anything.

Communicate—to keep the right information flowing in an acceptable way to those who need to hear it.

Troubleshoot—finding the problem and discerning its degree of concern. You need to know what has happened, why it happened, and how it affects the organization.

Problem solve—come up with creative solutions to problems in order to keep productivity at its peek.

Implement decisions and strategies—implementation is the action step that brings completion. Strategies identify and prioritize those steps.

Coordinate staff and tasks—know how to bring everyone into the vision with the same degree of understanding and commitment, and know how to coordinate their efforts.

Develop predictable processes—process is the step-by-step activity that keep the end result predictable.

Gather correct information—know where the information can be found, and collect what information is important at the time.

Plan successfully—understand what comes first and the necessary order of events to complete the goals.

Manage time—prioritize tasks, eliminate time-wasters, and deal with distractions efficiently. Take care of paperwork; don't get bogged down in it.

Take risks—Helen Keller said, "Avoiding danger is no safer in the long run than outright exposure. Life is either a daring adventure, or nothing."

Endure adversity—be unafraid to fail and willing to pay the price for success.

Accept criticism—no one likes criticism, but always listen and look for where you might be shortsighted about yourself.

Get results—you cannot stay in a leadership position long if you do not get results. Results are expected of you and are part of the game.

Navigating
the Second Chariot Road Map

If you hear a voice within you saying, "You cannot paint," then by all means paint, and that voice will be silenced.[9]

—VINCENT VAN GOGH

BESIDES SKILL AND character, a second in command must possess many of the qualities of the top executive. Many times the same skills are required because executive tasks are delegated from number one to number two with expectations that they will be carried out with the same excellence and results. These are, for the most part, leadership skills. Look at some of the qualities that you should focus on and develop to become an excellent number two. It takes courage to lead, and courageous leaders will always get their share of success. To navigate successfully, learn the following lessons.

YOU CAN'T GO THE WAY UNTIL YOU KNOW THE WAY

You should develop management skills as well as leadership skills. Many times leadership tells us "where," and management tells us "how." Leadership is *not* management. The two skills are distinctly different, and good leaders possess and use both. In order to move fast and get things done, you need to know how fast management can respond to leadership. By having management skills, you can give directions and actually know where those directions will take the organization. If you have to discover this by trial and error, you may still get there, but you won't be first. Mario Andretti once said, "If things seem under control, you are just not going fast enough."

Leadership is 90 percent inspiration and 10 percent information. Leaders direct by inspiring rather than dictating. They coach, encourage, and guide. Effective leaders discover with their team what has to be done. They determine, with their team members, what resources are needed to get the job done. The leaders then provide those resources and get out of the way so their people can perform.

Leaders use their heads and their hearts more than their backs and their hands. They see a vision for the future, and they gain perspective of the environment, of time, of risk, of synergy, and how they all will affect the organization. They understand the game plan and the talent on the team. They know what each position requires, who to put in each one, and who to call on when action is needed.

Get an understanding of the big picture. Great leaders see the big picture and the necessity of every player. When they do, they become more creative and better team players. They open opportunities for their people to do great things, to learn, to grow, to make a difference. These leaders share information and insights with their team so they also can see the big picture. Their followers gain a sense of purpose to their efforts, which makes work more fulfilling.

Great leaders cultivate the skills of their subordinate leaders by concentrating on people rather than on tasks. Results come when people are happy in their work environment and feel appreciated. It feels great to come to work under great leadership. People enjoy the experience and almost hate to go home at the end of the day. The organizational culture becomes favorable to high performance, safety, and health, and becomes a community of happy, satisfied people. Great leaders make people feel like they really belong. When leadership consistently expresses a high degree of caring and interest in their people, the result is that they connect. Emphasis must be placed on building and maintaining positive relationships, especially between employees and their immediate supervisors. A sense of teamwork and mutual concern grows from this attention—people helping each other because they want to, not just because it's their job.

Great leaders make sure everyone has the resources needed to perform at a high level. Those resources include information, tools, equipment, materials, time, space, and a supervisor to cut through red tape and remove any obstacles to high achievement.

Successful leaders provide their staff members with a wide range of opportunities for learning and for new experiences. Recognizing that people want to grow, they discover what will add value to each individual and help him or her attain that new skill. This not only helps personal growth, but eventually the new skill will benefit the organization. Successful leaders set the example by reading, attending seminars, and visiting other successful enterprises in their field. These leaders bring in experts from outside the company to train and share new ideas and fresh perspectives.

Compensate productivity with tangible rewards in addition to money. Compensation is important to all of us. The monetary issue will always be there. Top leaders accentuate the idea that other rewards are also important forms of compensation to employees. You can custom-make each compensation plan to fit the interests of each employee. Don't forget recognition, acknowledging a job done well.

Lay out your expectations for employees individually. Teach

them what results are necessary, and help them build a plan to get those results. With this knowledge, they are able to go confidently about their tasks, recruit the assistance they need, and make it happen.

Recognize that talent is not taught, but leadership and skills are. Take advantage of the talent people bring to the table, but know that it will not substitute for training and skill building. Skill does not replace talent, and talent does not replace skill. In the day-to-day operation, it is necessary that skills match the task. Talent may add a dimension of quickness or creativity, but skill is what produces results.

Because of the expectations that are put on the number-two leader, you must lead like number one "thinks" leaders should lead. Find out what those expectations are, and develop the skill set for navigating the second in command road map.

The Pie in the Eye Principle

As much as we would like to believe that every leader wants to see his subordinates developed and go on to have successful careers, it is just not always the case. However, the lack of interest in your success on the part of your leader is not an excuse for you not succeeding. The "pie in the eye" principle came to me while at lunch with a friend who was eating a piece of key lime pie and struggling under a "boss" that didn't really care about my friend's contribution to the organization. This boss only cared about the fact that he was boss.

The "pie in the eye" principle states: "Your bite of the pie, if it gets in your eye, does not justify your complaints." Your bite of the pie is the little corner of the office that you work in, under a boss who could care less about you, and who keeps you from seeing how big and great the opportunities for success are. Let's see what this means.

You have gifts, talent, experience, and brainpower. The boss in your department has relegated you to some menial task and uses his position to cast a long shadow over your potential.

Your value to the organization is hidden behind an insecure leader who has thrown some pie in your eye. Now you can't see beyond your dilemma.

Wipe the pie from your eye and see this: the bite is part of a slice that is part of a pie that is part of a meal that is on the table that is in the room that is part of the house that is part of the neighborhood that is part of the city that is part of the state that is part of the nation that is part of the continent that is part of the world that is part of the solar system that is part of the universe. It's a big world out there, but all you see is pie!

Don't worry about the bite of pie in your eye. Don't limit your life to that piece of the pie (your current situation). Rather look up and see how big life is and grab hold of the limitless opportunities available to people who work hard and refuse to be pigeon-holed by small people trying to hold on to their position.

Vincent Van Gogh once said, "If you hear a voice within you saying, 'You cannot paint,' then by all means paint, and that voice will be silenced."[10]

There are too many stories of great people who have had life throw pie in their eye only to overcome and accomplish great things. Helen Keller, Abe Lincoln, Lance Armstrong, and many more overcame affliction, disease, and defeat to become great. Consider the story of the "women of the Taliban."

You may have seen the public execution of a woman who was simply out in public with a man who was not her relative. This was filmed in a soccer field in Kabul, Afghanistan. These occurrences took place often under the cruel Taliban regime. Women were beaten with sticks by men if any part of their skin shown from under their burqas. They were not permitted to work or go to school and were considered under "house arrest" unless a male member of their family escorted them... even if they did not have a male in their family. They were denied immediate health care and were forbidden to listen to music and even fly kites. Ninety-seven percent suffered depression and stress.

During the rule of the Taliban many acts of violence and public executions were documented and videoed by...who else?...Afghan women who courageously hid cameras under their garments in order to give the world a record of their abuse.

The women of the Taliban are free for the most part today, and we pray for their total liberation. They are an example of people under the most limiting situations finding their place in the world by denying to be enslaved by cruel and ignorant leaders. We really don't have an excuse in America to live our lives pining in the corner feeling hopeless about our situation. No one limits our potential; we either create it or lose it.

Going From First to Second

Only the strong survive.[11]

—BILL STARR

WHEN YOU HAVE been the top executive in your own business, nonprofit, or ministry and have called the shots for years, what happens when you then become a subordinate? It may be harder to adjust downward than upward. It was a challenge to me to come in as a subordinate after years of leading my own organizations. The challenge did not come in the form of tasks or the size of the challenge, but rather in waiting for someone else to make the decision about what I would do and where I fit in. For the previous fifteen years, it had been me making the decisions, setting the timeline, and initiating the action steps. Now I had to wait on someone to tell me, in his own time, what my next step would be. Often he would tell me, change his mind, then stop the process altogether. It was a struggle for me at first. I did learn how to wait and eventually was able to teach others how to be productive while they waited for the next command to come down from headquarters.

Some of the temptations you will face once you leap to second place and the way you handle them will ultimately decide whether or not you succeed.

Here are several examples of the temptations we face every day.

In your zeal to prove yourself or get recognition, you can overstep your boundaries. You end up just talking about yourself and not the team. You can wear down the appreciation that others have for you if you constantly promote your own virtues. If you have any, others will see them.

You are the second in command of your department, division, or company, and you yearn to run the whole show. You ran enterprises before, so why not this one? You overstep your boundaries and cause division. Then you begin to pursue that coveted top position, thinking that you could do a better job, but that is not predictable. You may not do a better job. Besides, becoming number one is not a giant leap forward; it is a series of small steps.

Thirty-five years ago, history in space exploration was made. The moon received its first visitor...Neil Armstrong. When astronaut Neil Armstrong said the famous line "One small step for man, one giant leap for mankind," we were spellbound by such a simple but profound statement. Neil Armstrong did not leap to the moon; he simply stepped off the ladder of the landing module onto the surface of the moon. He took that one giant step, but think of the billions of small steps that preceded it. Remember, it doesn't start out as one giant leap; it starts out as one small step with many to follow.

A star number two doesn't always shine as a number one. You may desire the limelight, but remember, a whole generation of number-two executives washed out in America during the 1990s as CEOs because they didn't know what they lacked when they took over in times of crisis. They had experience in other industries as CEO, but that experience didn't translate in the new industry. They shined as number twos but were lackluster as number ones. Understanding the learning curve and how it will affect you is vitally important.

You are tempted to undermine the leadership of number one. You complain to the other subordinates about the leadership style of number one. You believe it will help everyone see your gifts and abilities. But this will have a negative impact on the enterprise that will negatively affect you in the end.

You only see the weaknesses of the boss. You are so focused on the perceived weaknesses or inconsistencies of the leader that you become slack in the performance of your own duties and fail to meet expectations. It is then that his/her strengths reveal themselves.

In the position of second in command, you are more subject to division. The second in command is more subject to bribes, disloyalty, usurping of authority, and the list goes on. Maintaining your integrity is huge.

You can be ignored if you do take the top job. When the second in command takes the primary leadership role, he is sometimes ignored, despised, and compared to his or her predecessor. All the sweetness is gone because you didn't pay the price for respect at the second level.

You want to lead for the wrong reason. The questions may be asked: Why do people want to be leaders? What is their priority? What personal benefit does one seek as a leader? Is it for the good of the enterprise or for your own ego?

Wrong motivations to control others plague many second in commands. This is a dangerous desire, as is the desire for monetary gain.

You don't have the same priorities as the boss. Your priorities would cause conflict because you see the "win" differently than the boss. Personal goals and reward pursuits conflict with the overall vision of the enterprise. A leader often bases decisions on a single priority, which may be conscious or unconscious.

This priority controls his leadership style and efficiency.

You become frustrated and quit. Now you are unemployed, cynical, and a perpetual complainer about how it should have been. But at least you are not alone—there are many people in the world just like you.

HOW TO START STRONG
AND STAY STRONG AS NUMBER TWO

There are skills necessary to being a good second in command. You should possess those skills when you arrive and learn more while you are there, but you should have some to get a good start. Nothing ensures success more than a strong start. Below are some insights to help you understand what you need to know.

Insights for staying strong

A second in command needs access to key players. Bring your subordinates into the loop. It could be the first time that they are closely involved in the leadership of the company. When you let those that serve you into the "circle" of influence and decision making, they will become your greatest assets in future endeavors.

Nurture strong relationships with the board of directors. This is a critical part of future success. During your initial months at the helm, you have to spend extra time having face-to-face meetings with board members to learn their views. The board is often the decision-making entity in an organization, and without their support you may be facing an uphill battle with every new idea you want to initiate.

Executives urge seconds in command to seek wide responsibilities—and to learn as much as possible about important areas in which they don't have direct authority. Knowledge gaps make it harder on everyone when a new number two takes the helm. Learn what is necessary for you to become a positive contributor as soon as possible.

Don't let your ego get hung up on doing everything yourself.

Delegating responsibility to others helps build the team. Not only that, but it also helps prepare those under you to take over tasks you will not have time for later. Make sure that you delegate to develop as many of your subordinates as possible.

Don't look at yourself as number one's errand runner. You may be implementing someone else's strategy, but treat it as your personal quest for success. Make your position work for the good of everyone, including you. You are an integral part of the success plan. Understand the vital nature of what you do, or you may not perform to the high level expected or needed by the organization.

Learn how number one likes to be communicated to. A great challenge that needs to be addressed by seconds in command is lack of feedback from the top. Some primary leaders are very hard to communicate with. Be creative in this. Use e-mail, fax, and notes; send messages through their personal assistants. Try to keep the lines of communication open. Find out how number one likes to communicate and do it her way. One word of advice, however: don't ask too many "I don't know" questions. Number one may think you don't know enough about your job and that you can't do it. Research as much as you can and come up with as many answers as possible on your own. Remember, the one that has the most information leads.

There is a quantum leap between having the ultimate responsibility and having someone else above you to test your ideas on and who guides you as to what to do. It can be a comfort to know that the "buck" does not stop with you. Get as much input from number one as you can.

Win in the leadership meeting. One thing to know is how to lead a staff meeting with other leaders. You can have great ideas but lose opportunity if you can't back up those ideas in a meeting with other leaders. They may have reasons why your idea won't work, and unless you can counter their reasons, your idea is dead on arrival. Here are some keys to winning in the leadership meeting.

1. *Whoever has the most information leads the meeting.* First, you should strive to have the most current information on the subject. If you just sit in a meeting with no new ideas or information that would benefit your point of view, someone else will lead the meeting. It is possible that it will be someone who is most negative. Many times leadership is by default.

2. *Meet before you meet.* You should have had the "meeting before the meeting" to have the necessary support you need. If others are already on board with your idea, it will not be so hard to sell. Too often we wait to reveal our great idea about the necessary steps or changes we need to take, and everyone is taken off guard. You have no one to vouch for the brilliance of your new plan, so it flops. When others have had the chance to hear you out, ask questions, and then help you make the adjustments that will give your idea broad appeal, you are bound to win.

3. *Be first to write down the idea.* Write the first draft of the proposed change or new task. The writer of the first draft often shapes the ensuing discussion; everyone else is then responding to your ideas. The writer of the first draft gets the first say in things.

Keys to Being a Successful Second in Command

A crucial ingredient in any specific relationship involving a leader and a second in command is that they complement each other. If these two people don't have complementary roles and gifts, the relationship is unlikely to work. For a number two to be successful as a strong leader within an organization, he has to have a distinct role and distinct set of responsibilities; otherwise he can easily turn into a staff assistant. When this happens, the number-two role often becomes political and spreads politics throughout an organization because it is based on an artificial organizational position rather than meaty responsibilities.

Another key is unselfishness. The number two will accomplish a lot of work that the leader will get credit for, and that has to be OK. He has to be a secure person whose focus is on what is accomplished rather than on who gets credit. Sometimes a retired CEO will do well in this kind of role—he has accomplished his personal goals and achieved all the recognition he needs and can forgo it if there's a goal he wants to help his boss work toward.

This gives a third key: believing in the goal. If you're committed to a goal and that goal is more important than you are, it's much easier to accept the relative anonymity of being in a subordinate role if that role can enable you to make a real contribution.

A final key is good judgment. Frequently a number-one/number-two structure occurs when a visionary leader realizes that he needs a detail person to run the operation. This also makes the number two a mediator between the leader and the rest of the organization. Visionary leaders generally have lots of bad ideas (it's part of the price we pay for the good ones), and they need someone who has the ability to distinguish between the good ideas and the bad ones. Often the rank-and-file employees will recognize an idea as bad, and their displeasure will filter upward. The number two has to be good at sensing these things and faithfully bringing them forward. Otherwise the leader can get increasingly detached from reality. Of course, for the number two to keep the leader honest in this way requires openness and trust on the part of the leader. The number two has to make sure he is wise in helping the leader see the obstacles clearly without being obstructionist in his approach.

WorldCom provides a great example of how a number two can fail his leader. Bernie Ebbers was a classic visionary; his chief financial officer, Scott Sullivan, was a detail man. But when WorldCom's business started to deteriorate, rather than force Ebbers to face the music, Sullivan resorted to changing the numbers so profits looked the way everyone thought they should. This approach caused the company's path to become increasingly self-destructive. By the time everyone realized what had happened, the hole was too deep to climb out of, and the company filed for bankruptcy.

THE ROLE AND THE REWARD

Personally, being a number two helped me clarify what I was working toward. If you feel that God had assigned you to contribute to a specific effort, realize that it shouldn't matter what your title is. God is going to judge you according to whether you used the gifts He gave you in the way He intended for them to be used. It shouldn't matter, then, what your title is. Absorb the truth that you can put aside any struggle for recognition because God will one day provide the "last word," and it is He who hands out the rewards.

MAKING MISTAKES

Get used to it; you will make mistakes in any position that you are in. But there are some mistakes that you need to avoid.

One key mistake we make is publicly expressing disagreement with the leader. It's kind of like parents with their children. All parents are going to have some disagreements on how to handle certain things with their kids, no matter how like-minded they are. If they're wise, parents will work through these things together privately so that they always present a united front to the children. Otherwise, the children will learn to play one against the other.

It's the same in any organization. The leader and the number two need to work through any disagreements privately so that they always present unity to the organization. Otherwise, political maneuvering will quickly creep in, and when that happens the effectiveness of any organization is greatly diminished.

Also, never blindside the leader with information or problems that he is unable to respond to intelligently in the meeting. He should be not be perceived as being ill-informed or out of the loop in front of staff. Always give critical information to the leader either before or after the meeting, unless, of course, the meeting is being held for the purpose of divulging such information.

8

Insights From the Second Chariot

If you succeed in helping others win, you win.

—AUTHOR

B EFORE I ENUMERATE some things the second chariot needs to know to be fulfilled, it is important to point out what the view is from behind the "lead chariot." Depending on who the boss is, the view could be one of fast-moving, decisive action that brings victory after victory, or it could be one of confusion, exclusion, and redoing of failed attempts at success. It can be a view of hope and a great future, or it can be one of disappointment and lost hope for improvement and advancement.

The view from the second chariot does not have to be from the rear, however. When the first chariot has the wisdom and the prudence to pull you alongside so you can see what he sees, you will get a better view of where he is going and how best to assist him in getting there—not to mention being able to see the dangers that lie ahead. Being in a position at the side of the first chariot gives you his perspective and allows him to glean from your wisdom and experience.

Second place has the image of "not quite good enough to be number one." It can even mean *loser,* as in this saying, "Second place is the first loser." In this American entrepreneurial society there is the mind-set that our ambition should always be for the top job. Many CEOs and company presidents have heard these words from younger emerging leaders: "I want your job!" We all tend to arrive at a new position with the attitude, "I have no experience, but I'm willing to start at the top." But many labor for years in the bowels of an organization before they see promotion. So if you think of yourself as a leader, how can you exert influence and make a difference?

Truth is, if they had the boss's job, most people would probably fall flat on their faces. Everyone is not meant to be at the top of the organizational chart. Someone has to fill the lower levels of the chart, and these lower-level fillers need to have talent and great leadership ability if the organization is to succeed.

For many years I worked as the number-one man nationally and internationally and did OK. My greatest successes came, however, when I worked in subordinate roles. In the last fourteen years, having worked as the second in command, I can honestly say that I have accomplished more, had greater success, and enjoyed far more influence. One of the most obvious reasons for this was the availability of resources.

As the top-level executive, you don't always have the opportunity to develop new alliances or experience new avenues as you do in the position of second chariot. The second chariot is a key position that the majority possesses. Remember, most people assist someone else—you might be second to a second or second to a third, but the principles of being successful as the second in command still apply.

Smart second-in-command leaders recognize that leadership is an attitude and not just a position. They understand that they are there to complement number one and help him perform his role with success. They also know that leadership must come from many levels and that their level is as important as any other.

To be effective in your position as number two, you must develop your leadership ability before you can exercise influence in the organization. Because leadership is influence, it is influence that will bring you success when dealing with others. Since your goal is to raise the productivity of everyone in the organization, and not to just possess a title, focus on influence and you will win.

Recognition will come with success. Define the "who" that needs to know that you are being successful and keep them in the "results" loop. As you serve to make others successful, your success will grow and you will be noticed.

UNDERSTAND THE RESOURCE ENVIRONMENT

R.R.E.—Resource Rich Environment

Many subordinate leaders experience success when they are immersed in an environment that is replete with resources. Only when resources are available in the areas of finance, human resources, networking, and influence do they find success in the number-two position. This can take place in numerous scenarios. Therefore, before leaving your second-in-command position to launch out on your own, make sure there will be resources where you are going. Examples: when there is a venture capitalist in place to help you get started, when another company is well resourced in all areas, or when there is a good network of people who believe in you and will help you resource what you intend to do. Otherwise, it may be best to either remain where you are or wait until resources avail themselves to you.

R.V.E.—Resource Void Environment

The other reality is that when seconds in command move out on their own to be their own boss, they sometimes move into a situation void of the resources they had while in the number-two spot. While with the company, in the number-two position, there were human, financial, and networking resources from which they could draw. Now, all alone, they have to start over to rebuild the resource base. Too many times it just isn't possible, and they languish. Later you often find them working again with a different company in a subordinate role because they could never gather the necessary resources to make it on their own.

Resource Transfer

When you make the move from second in command in one company to first in command in another company, or in a self-employed situation, be sure to bring the necessary resources with you. This is called "resource transfer." It is simply making sure that you have similar resources at your disposal in your next position as you did in your previous situation where you enjoyed success.

RESOURCE ENVIRONMENT ILLUSTRATION:
THINGS SECOND IN COMMAND NEEDS TO KNOW

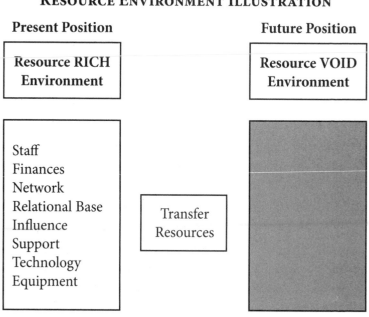

RESOURCE ENVIRONMENT ILLUSTRATION

Present Position

Resource RICH
Environment

Future Position

Resource VOID
Environment

Staff
Finances
Network
Relational Base
Influence
Support
Technology
Equipment

Transfer
Resources

> Resources are vital to the success of any person or business.

> In order to ensure success in a future position you must make sure the resources you need are there.

Know your strengths and weaknesses.

Don't inflate your value. Overestimating how much you're worth could devalue your personal stock. Titles have the tendency to "hyper-inflate" your estimation of your worth. Know your failings and shortcomings as well as your strengths. You will fail sometimes, so prepare your boss for the inevitable.

Someone said, "Half of being smart is to know what you are dumb about."

Know which gifts you possess and which ones you don't. The way to learn what gifts you possess is to listen to the positive things people say to you. For instance, if people say, "You are a great communicator," or, "You really know how to make people feel comfortable and accepted," then ask yourself, "Is this my gift?"

If you are told this over and again, then just accept it as your gift and begin improving on it. But don't make the mistake of thinking you have a gift in some area if other people can't see it. It is probable that you do not possess gifts if they are not visible to others.

Be dedicated to learning. Learning is the only thing that ensures growth, and it continually expands the realms of your potential. You can become greater, more useful to the enterprise, more adept in your performance, and strengthen any weakness you have if you commit to being a learner. John Wooden, former UCLA coach, puts it like this: "It's what you learn after you know it all that counts."[12] If you think you know it all, that's it—that's the end of your growth. I know many people who are know-it-alls and are not open to new information. Their usefulness to the organization is limited. One example of this stands out in my mind.

A student from a Bible college called and wanted an appointment with me to get some ideas of what he should do once he graduated. We sat and talked for a half-hour. He shared some of what he was doing and his vision and goals. I listened and responded in a way that I thought would be helpful and give him some direction. Later, in an e-mail, he rejected the things I had shared with him and scolded me for not living up to his expectations of me as a leader. He could have been right—I may have failed him in that thirty-minute window of time that our lives intersected. But unless he changes, his unwillingness to accept new information that is contrary to his belief system will be his downfall.

My experience has been that some people think years ahead of everyone else in certain fields. Rejecting their ideas could amount to getting behind the learning curve and ending up a latecomer into the new reality. You need new information in order to lead from any position, especially from the number-two spot.

Leading from the second chariot requires skills for making hard decisions that involve many people, personalities, and attitudes. It draws criticism, jealousy, and envy. It is a major responsibility for someone with nerves of steel and stable emotions. You can neither get mad nor be passive—it is a balancing act. Stay up to the task by judging yourself honestly and getting feedback from reliable sources.

Don't sell yourself short either. Keep your strengths and weaknesses in balance, and be objective. Know when you can confidently move forward, and know when you must say, "I don't know how to do this!" The lead chariot needs to know this about you so that he won't have the wrong expectations of you. You must stay in the frame of mind that you have a lot to learn, but let yourself be influenced and challenged to grow. Knowing who you are, the good and the not-so-good, is part of building a strong self-image built on truth and self-understanding.

Focus on strengths and learn to overcome your weaknesses. (First, break all the rules.) Learn to delegate tasks to someone who is better at it than you and don't let pride set a trap for you. You are not the best at everything.

Make sure someone is in the wings to take up the task if necessary or build a team to help you. Your worth to the organization is defined by the value you bring and measured by productivity, relationships, influence, and profitability.

> ❭ *Leadership insight:* Learn from others' mistakes. You will not live long enough to make them all yourself.

> ❭ *Management insight:* Delegate in order to develop others in your team. There will always be things that

you don't need to do but others need to learn to do. This builds the competency of the team and keeps you out of hot water.

> *Relational insight:* Humility produces a greater degree of success for the second in command than an overinflated ego. Understanding your own frailties and weaknesses helps you understand the shortcomings of those who follow you.

Know the leader and where he expects to go.
Your goals and destination must change with the needs and vision of the first chariot. Knowing his own priorities helps him meet his goals and live up to his expectations of himself and of others to whom he is accountable. After all, that is why he hired you.

To do this effectively, you must share ownership of his goals. Be sure not to become competitive with the boss. Pressure to perform can cause you to become competitive and cause the boss to fear emergent leadership. Share his goals, and work to help him reach those goals. Loyalty is number one, not number two. This gives him the support he needs to aspire to greater things and perhaps leaves a vacuum that you can fill someday.

You need to communicate three things to the boss in word and action. First, "I have a purpose that is not going to interfere with your purpose. It will interface with it." Next, "I have a calling that is not going to negate your calling. It will enhance it." Finally, "I have a dream that is not going to eclipse your dream. It will emerge from it."

The bosses may be wrong, but they are still the bosses. Understand them!

Understand your boss's personality traits and what is normal for him or her. Be able to explain to other subordinates how number one is different, and help them understand his mode of operation. Some folks think that trying to understand or putting themselves in the boss's shoes or situation is playing politics, but that is far from the truth. It is skillful maneuvering of your chariot. When you have a complete understanding of the boss's issues and concerns, you are on the right page. If you create good rapport with number one and sensitivity to his/her concerns, the credibility you have will increase as well as the attention of that lead chariot. This includes understanding his/her MO—how she thinks, how he leads change, and how she handles criticism.

The scapegoat—"A scapegoat is nearly as welcomed as a solution to the problem."

Some first-chariot leaders are very secure and will extend trust and even take up for a subordinate if a problem arises or if there is a failure. Some, on the other hand, will find someone to blame, a scapegoat. I have worked for both kinds. One was very secure and always trying to help those who failed to get back on their feet and continue. The other, especially if it reflected on him, would find a scapegoat and put the failure as far from himself as he could. His insecurity and fear of failure caused many innocent employees to be afraid of retribution when something went wrong. Heads would roll, job descriptions would change, and others would be sitting in your desk taking over your position. This is how some leaders handle mistakes.

Knowing how your leader handles change is also important. Some are very concerned for the welfare of the workforce and want to keep as many in the game as possible. These leaders will coach the staff through change to make sure that everyone can adjust to it and keep a positive attitude. Others will denigrate your position and what you are doing to the point that you wonder why the organization ever hired you for that job to start with. It is their way of forcing you to accept change. One way or the other, you will have to flow with every change that is made.

Know what to expect when change comes; know also that change will come more frequently than you thought. I know that too much change can be detrimental to an organization if it does not have clear direction. The fact is that when you lead the team down too many dead ends, the team will end up in "neutral" as far as productivity is concerned. As a second in command, it is your job to help the leader make the right changes at the right time and to realize that much of the time change is good and a must.

Think like the lead chariot! Read the same books; breathe the same air; look from the same glasses; understand her goals; know her issues and concerns as the boss. You should know your boss's top three goals. They should be the road map for your job and those who follow you. If not, you will have a very tough ride. Your future in the organization will depend on how well you are able to look at and feel the vision of the lead chariot. If you can do that and buy into all he sees, you will no doubt be vital to the organization and a true second in command. You don't have to agree with every detail of the vision, but the essence is important. Be willing to make contributions even though they are not in the way that you first thought you would. Some of your greatest offerings may never be noticed. However, you should always be on the lookout for other avenues to make those offerings to the corporation and to your boss. You may just get an opportunity to do so after all.

Look out for the lead chariot, because she does not always see the pitfalls. One important task of the second chariot is to always look for potential problem areas and find ways to avoid them. This is a troubleshooter role that many second chariots play in organizations.

> *Leadership insight:* Vision is the ability to see. As a leader, you are in a position to see further than anyone else. Get others to help you discern what you are looking at.

> *Management insight:* Communicate to your peers and subordinates an accurate description of what the

leader and you are seeing. The clearer the picture in the minds of the workforce, the better chance that there will be a correct appraisal and response to the situation.

> *Relational insight:* Never set up a friend for failure or embarrassment. "With friends like that, who needs enemies?" Ever hear that one? When you set up a friend to be embarrassed or to fail at something, in reality you act as her enemy. Never allow a friend, colleague, relative, or anyone else to walk into a situation where they will get "whacked" if you have the power to stop them or the situation.[13]

Know when to challenge ideas and strategies, and when to roll.

This is the "challenge and roll" principle. I used it all the time to help keep my leader from making mistakes. But often, after challenging an idea, I would have to roll and accept his decision. Never challenge the leader personally. Often you will find out that you are dead wrong. It would have been embarrassing to win the argument only to lead the team to failure. Trust that the leader has a feel for what is taking place, and don't go too far out on a limb for the sake of "being heard." It is best sometimes just to sit and listen. Maybe a better idea will come.

Be keenly aware of the values of the organization, and stay within those parameters. With the right strategy, even values can be "redefined" for the good of the changing direction of the organization. Sometimes you can challenge ideas if you think better options are available to the leader, but don't be dogmatic or unyielding. What you think is best for the organization may not be at that particular time. Remember that the leader is in that position because of his abilities and decision-making prowess. You can create suspicion if you challenge every idea or try to change to "better" strategies without letting the leader try his idea first.

> *Leadership insight:* "It is better to keep your mouth shut and appear stupid than to open it and remove all doubt."[14]   —Mark Twain

> *Management insight:* Brainstorming is a tool to create information; the more information you have, the better possibility of a great decision.

> *Relational insight:* Know that it is better to have been found right than to be proven wrong.

Know what the first chariot needs and what he wants for the company and himself.

Know how to give him what he needs and wants. Needs are nonnegotiable many times, but wants always give him more satisfaction. Meeting the needs goals without satisfaction makes for a very weary endeavor. Wants could be the monetary and personal rewards that give the journey a feel of fulfillment.

Needs are the nuts and bolts that hold the organization together; screws come in afterward to shore up loose parts. These are the wants. We see what the end results should be and know the steps to get there, but the wants are added to make it rich in reward and satisfaction. When the screws come loose, desire can get rattled and the reward factor can be lost. Make sure that wants line up with needs and reach for both.

> *Leadership insight:* "Winners can tell you where they are going, what they plan to do along the way, and who will be sharing the adventure with them."[15]
> —Denis Waitley

> *Management insight:* "Management is doing things right; leadership is doing the right things."[16]
> —Peter F. Drucker

> *Relational insight:* After obvious needs are met and satisfied, the real needs emerge. A hungry person

does not know she is lonely until she has eaten and
is full.

Know what makes the enterprise successful and produce it.

The key components for success in every organization are
different. You must take ownership of every component, every
phase of every department, to meet the goals of the leader and
his organization.

The measuring sticks the leader looks at when gauging his
success are net profit, growth that meets expectations, time-
lines, and personnel performance reports. Positive response
by the public to new products or services may also play an
important role. Therefore, it is imperative that you see the
importance of each piece and work on all fronts for success.
This requires seeing the "big picture." The big picture is the
overall plan, how it is to be implemented, and what you can do
to get the organization all the way to the win.

The successful subordinate leader must look at things from
the perspectives of several people, not just from his perch on
the corporate ladder. You must undoubtedly have the perspective of the first chariot, but also the perspective from those
behind you. Listen for the "horses" behind you, and make
sure that they are following closely. You should also work for
the success of everyone that follows you. Their success is your
success, even if they seem to get all the attention. Sooner or
later, with everyone else, you will get your reward.

When you know what needs to be done and can't see the creative catalyst in the organization, *you* must be that catalyst. The
boss must have someone who can bring the creative process
into the forefront to pave the way for the next move the organization needs to make. Without creative thinking, the organization will fall behind in its ability to remain competitive.

Be a doer! Doers may make mistakes, but they always get
things done. John Wooden has said, "The athlete who says
that something cannot be done should never interrupt the one

who is doing it."[17]

How do you know when you are successful as number two? When you have helped your department, organization, and primary leader reach their goals and realize the completion of their vision of success. When you see people developed to the point that they are built into a productive organization and they have gained new skills and experience. When you are confident that you can organize, delegate, plan, and build strategic systems and structures that can overcome challenges and reach goals as a team. When number one is free to dream and promote vision and number two is trusted to make those dreams come true through his organizational skills as he gets the best from his team.

> *Leadership insight:* Nothing is more successful than success itself.

> *Management insight:* Manage people for success by helping the organization reach its goals, one employee at a time.

> *Relational insight:* Let your subordinates shine. If they shine bright enough, it will reflect on you. I have learned that the main responsibility I have in my relationships with my subordinates is to make each one look as good as possible. The better they look, the better I look. It is my quest then to empower, train, encourage, and put them in the place where they can shine the most. Everybody wins![18]

Know his limits and when to draw the line.

As we talked about earlier, the second chariot should take ownership of the vision, but be careful not to take more than you can deliver. The excitement of a new task or challenge is exhilarating and puts a fire in your belly. You jump at the opportunity to do something bigger, and into the fire you go. But fire in the belly could end up burning out the stove! Only accept responsibilities where there is the expertise to do it or the opportunity to build the right team to do it. I often accept responsibilities knowing that the only way they will get done is if I can pull the right team together. Wisdom would teach you that you should only accept a task if you can build a team to work with you to accomplish that task.

Be sure to understand what the expectations are from the first chariot when you accept a new task. You may be better off delegating the task to someone who is more experienced and better at it than you. One of my favorite mottos is: "If you want to get something done, and get it done right, *get someone else to do it.*" I have discovered that no matter how much I know, someone else always knows more about the subject than I do and can do the job better than I can. Accept the responsibility, delegate the task, and keep the person accountable. But let him do it! It is reasonable to accept the fact that the first chariot will ask you to do things beyond your realm of expertise. So, find others in the organization to fulfill those obligations. You can't tell the boss no, but you don't have to do everything alone or yourself. Another motto of mine is: "Nothing is impossible for the man who does not have to do it himself!"

> *Leadership insight:* As a leader it is your responsibility to make the organization successful, not to gain fame. However, if success is achieved, you will be the one to get the credit, and fame will come.

> *Management insight:* Delegation is the art of recognizing that there are more gifted people around you and utilizing them for the benefit of the enterprise.

> *Relational insight:* Live for the success of others, and you'll be successful.

Know how to lead as well as how to follow.

It is important to have a 360-degree view of the organization's structure and each department's needs. This is corporate "peripheral vision." You should be aware of the new talent the company needs and watch for and develop those emerging leaders. Don't leave the subordinates in your dust. You will always need them to carry out the tasks delegated to you, and they deserve respect. Keeping them abreast of necessary changes in direction, goals, and strategies keeps them on your team. The synergy created by this kind of "team" approach assures success nearly every time.

Understand the condition of the "flock," and communicate to them and care for them. Share this information with the first chariot. When support fails, the top falls. Rosanne Badowski, former personal assistant to General Electric's CEO, Jack Welch, puts it this way, "Be bilingual—understand and be able to use the language of staff above and below you."[19]

Listen for the horses behind you, and make sure they are following closely. On a few occasions, the employees will understand the directive of the lead chariot, but they will fail to follow closely enough due to a wait-and-see approach. They have been down too many dead-end streets and are tentative, afraid to commit. They just don't buy into the changes. The problem with this approach is that they may be wrong! This may be the road they have been looking for. This directive or this vision may be the one that changes the total direction of the enterprise and leads it to its win. If this happens, the rest of the team is out of sync and has to run hard to catch up. Make certain that you, as the second chariot, keep the rest of the team close to that lead chariot. However, if the lead chariot runs too fast and the other horses fall too far back, let the lead chariot know about it so he can adjust. He must be kept abreast of the facts about the organization. Don't keep the fact that buy-in has not happened a secret.

Change is inevitable, so help your followers adapt to the change. Often the world outside is changing faster than the world inside the company, with no end in sight. This means that change is coming to the company. Make sure that you condition them for change and teach them how to exist and thrive in the new "get it done" culture. Then, when the direction changes, they won't have to steer quite so hard or travel so far to end up at the same ultimate destination.

Often your subordinates find themselves in difficult situations and have to make critical decisions. Make "heavy" decisions for them. That is why you are in your position. Use your experience and wisdom to help your followers make the right decision at the right time. This is "peripheral vision." Peripheral vision allows you to see the primary leader as well as the others in subordinate roles. Otherwise, those trying to follow you lose direction and stray off course. This only makes your task harder.

Create a culture where you provide upward mobility to those following you by helping develop them to carry greater responsibilities. It can become a culture to help promote every person in the company as he or she grows and develops. By doing this, you help the entire organization reach its goals. This also helps overcome suspicion and infighting. Through communication, teamwork, and appreciating each other's gifts, you set the stage for cooperation and unity. People will support a world they help create.

Remember, often the qualifications for the first and second chariots are nearly the same. There has to be trust and respect first; then come acceptance and admiration. Work for the respect you get from those you lead; give respect to those that follow like it is owed to them.

The middle child: The second chariot is like the "middle child" in a family. She has to have a strong working relationship with the one in front and the one in the back. She should be sensitive to the needs of both, be the mouthpiece for both, and be best friends to both. I learned this by observing my daughter Trudy. Trudy was sandwiched between her sisters Tammy and Shary. It seems that she had to share twice as much, talk twice as much, and had twice as many competitors.

Through it all, she gained collaboration skills and learned how to get along with people in difficult situations. She also learned when to give in and when to hold her turf.

The second in command leader is the communicator both up and down the corporate or familial ladder. In the same way that the first chariot is, in most situations, the big-picture, strategic visionary person, the second chariot generally has to be the strategy implementer. The second in command has to come up with the strategy to carry out the vision, get buy-in from all those below him, and inspire everyone to work toward the goal. It is when the dreamer and implementer are working as one that they bring all that follow them into the promised land of productivity and success.

As the second in command, you have to learn how to keep the "pack" together. You cannot allow the team members behind you to become disgruntled and alienated. You do this by keeping them in the game on decisions and in carrying out strategy. People support a world they help create. Honor all team members by letting them share in the rewards and giving them credit when they deserve it.

> *Leadership insight:* A leader can be defined as someone who is in the position to "take action" and actually does. "Leadership is action, not position."[20]
> —Davy Crockett

> *Management insight:* Good managers will have to recruit, delegate, train, motivate, manage, assist, and reward people to help them accomplish their goals. In other words, they must be good leaders.

> *Relational insight:* You have two arms—one to reach forward, one to reach back.

Keep the lead chariot informed about the health and attitude of the organization.

When you are the lead chariot, your visibility is impaired.

The lead chariot is responsible for seeing the present, past, and future. Sometimes the here and now suffers because of details. Those fine points are usually what end up affecting the attitudes of those in the company in a negative way. If those attitudes are not addressed, performance suffers and the organization begins to erode from within. This happens sometimes without the knowledge of the lead person. The second chariot should be that barometric pressure gauge to the rest of the organization, especially when the organization is large.

I have a friend who was a president of a toy company who says, "The toy business was simple. Five important things: the right product, for the right age child, in the hands of the right customers, at the right profitable cost, at the right time." The attitude of the organization, if wrong, could turn a *simple* business like that into a nightmare. Attitude in the organization is most important, so don't let it go bad. Stay on top of it.

If you have to be the bearer of the bad news, do it with grace, understanding the impact on the boss and the company. Some world leaders killed the messenger with bad news—look what happened with Stalin, Hitler, and others. They created their own blind spots and were most responsible for their own fall. Eventually the bad news they didn't want to hear was their undoing. It is vitally important that bad news get communicated to the lead chariot. It should come after you have thought about the pros and cons and some alternative solutions as well as an action plan that takes care of the issue of the day. Those who don't want to be in the second chariot will come into their supervisor's office, throw out the bad news, and leave. Do this with wisdom and tact, giving the lead guy a plan of attack. Yes, the lead guy is paid to hear the bad news. However, don't dwell on it or let him be its sole owner.

> ❯ *Leadership insight:* Bad news given with the right attitude and with a positive prognosis can be more useful than good news given nonchalantly.

❭ *Management insight:* Information is knowledge that is derived from experience, study, or instruction. The right information at the right time can be the difference between success and failure.

❭ *Relational insight:* Don't hold back truth. Truth, though sometimes hard to face, is liberating. Once the truth has been established in a given situation, all parties involved can discover the right thing to do. However, when you go along in life never really knowing the truth about your circumstances or what is interfering with a relationship, you will never resolve the difficulties. When conflicts go unresolved because truth is veiled, there is never the sense of closure. When truth is manipulated or finessed, you have nontruth…false assumptions. By allowing someone to believe the wrong thing about something you said or allowing misunderstanding to remain uncorrected, you set the stage for the propagation of false assumptions. Clear up every issue with truth, and you will have peace in your life and in the relationship.[21]

Be willing to accept that riding in the first chariot may not be your destiny.

There are other areas where you can be number one! Be number one in serving, caring, innovation, creativity, and in relationships. Be number one as a father, a mother, a spouse, and a friend. These are just as important as sitting in the front office. There is joy in all of these as well as in being a success corporately.

It is extremely rewarding to help set and attain goals that make the corporation and CEO successful. After all, what you accomplish is first seen by yourself, your family, and God. Afterward comes the recognition of your peers. Many times in my life, while working as the second in command in an organization, my wife or daughter or son-in-law would see my effort and dedication. They would know the contribution I made for the success of the organization and say something to me to let me know that they were watching and could see. Some friend or colleague would observe a job well done and mention it to me. They were proud of my achievements even though someone else might have gotten the credit. Best of all, God sees all that you do.

Remember, though you are not in the first chariot, as a team you can all be in first place. Success to the team is just as important, if not more important, as success to the leader. Without team success, there is no success for the leader. The experience of winning as a team can be rewarding enough, if you are secure in the position you play, to be fulfilled for a lifetime.

> *Leadership insight:* Getting the score requires a team effort. In the game, the leadership mysteriously passes from one player to the other. The one that calls the play gets things started, but the results are left up to the ability and leadership of the rest of the players.

> *Management insight:* Training each member of the team to perform at maximum potential is the only guarantee of success for the leadership.

> *Relational insight:* The camaraderie of a team is only present when each team member plays his part. In such cases, camaraderie can build strong, long-lasting friendships.

You must know when to walk and when to run.

Did you marry well? The first realization may be that no matter how much you work and accomplish, it never seems to please or impress the primary leader. No matter how much you want to work for an organization or how much you feel you have to offer, sometimes it just isn't a good match. There may never be a perfect match, and you will always have to work on the relationship. But some corporate cultures and personalities just don't match.

Know when to walk. When you can no longer give your heart to the organization and its vision and goals, it may be time to walk away. This is totally acceptable if you do it correctly. Leave in peace, and protect the ones that followed you and will be staying on. There will be times, though, when you must leave because you cannot grow anymore in the place where you work. Even more of a reason to move on is that you have accomplished what you came there to do. In these cases, look for new horizons. Remember, no one is concerned about your career path but you. If you are doing a good job, the boss will not want you to leave, but other factors may compel you to go. Make a commitment that if you are regularly being humiliated or put under pressure because you're given all the responsibility and none of the authority, you will make a choice: (a) try to change the system; (b) stay and get sick; or (c) leave.

Another sign that it may be time to walk away is when you are never allowed to operate in your strengths, when your gifts are ignored. This is the proverbial square peg in a round hole. If your supervisors cannot see your strengths and how they can benefit the organization, you will never be happy there. Either move into a position where you can use your gifts freely and function where you have strengths, or find a job where you can.

Know when to run. Unethical or dishonest business practices are your one-way ticket out the door. There is no good reason to stay with a company or a boss that is defrauding others or is dishonest to you. Neither money nor loyalty is a good enough reason to stay. Exit! Run! Run when illegal or unethical things are taking place, regardless of who your boss is. No one deserves that kind of loyalty. Here is a typical regret of people who stayed too long or did the wrong things: "I should have left sooner." Common regrets that many people have are a result of negative if not severe consequences for continuing something that they should have stopped sooner: "I should have quit smoking," they say, when they discover they have lung cancer. "I should never have left my spouse," they say, when they find out the second or third person they married is far less the person that their first spouse was. "I should have taken better care of myself," when they find out that they need triple bypass surgery.

Chuck Colson's lesson in staying too long.

Chuck Colson was the most powerful man in the Nixon White House after Halderman and Ehrlichman. He was in charge of communications.

Colson knew no limits in his dedication to achieving the reelection of Richard Nixon in 1972. He knew, of course, all about Watergate and the maneuverings that were going on, including a safe full of illicit and illegal money. He was in it up to his eyebrows. And at the time, morality and the virtues of integrity and honor were not strong points in Colson's life.

His failure is typical of people that get into power. They become drunk with it, live in a cocoon, work themselves into a stupor, and lose all perspective on the world. All they know is the intimate and horribly dynamic circle in which they exist. They kill themselves working fifteen- and eighteen-hour days, seven days a week, fifty-two weeks a year, and they do it for years on end! They are consumed with working in proximity to people of influence, wealth, and power. After all, Colson was aide to the president of the United States. This unconditional dedication blinds you to wrongdoing—you get caught up in it and can no longer discern when it is time to exit. The morality of the moment is, "Whatever advances the cause of the leader, do it!"

Colson was guilty. He was just as much a victim as a player. But he stayed too long, and it cost him. He paid with a jail term for his part in the Watergate scandal. Had he known when to run, it could have saved him from many sorrows.

Chuck Colson has become a born-again Christian. He served time and deserved to do so, but now he has redeemed his life by the time and effort that he puts into a nationwide prison ministry.

Another man involved in Watergate shares his insights about the plight one faces when he gets caught up in wrong-doing for what he believes is the right thing. John Ehrlichman learned a great lesson. One of those convicted in the Watergate scandals of the early 1970s, Ehrlichman wrote that upon his release from prison, he found himself at a very low ebb. He began to take stock of his life:

> Every day I read the Bible, walked on the beach, and sat in front of my fireplace thinking and sketching, with no outline or agenda. I had no idea where all this was leading or what answers I'd find. Most of the time, I didn't even know what the questions were. I just watched and listened. I was wiped out. I had nothing left that had been of value to me—honor, credibility, virtue, recognition, profession—nor did I have the allegiance of my family. I had managed to lose that too.
>
> Since about 1975 I have begun to learn to see myself. I care what I perceive about my integrity, my capacity to love and be loved, and my essential worth.... Those interludes, the Nixon episodes in my life, have ended. In a paradoxical way, I'm grateful for them. Somehow I had to see all of that and grow to understand it in order to arrive at the place where I find myself now.[22]

Know that some of the factors that keep you on the job are not measured in monetary terms.

Some factors that lead to dissatisfaction in the workplace are not related to pay and benefits.

The no-fun factor. You can't stay in a place where you aren't happy. Being unhappy on the job can cause problems at home. A man or woman who dreads going to work will eventually pass that unhappy attitude to the rest of the family. If your job isn't fun, look for something that is. It will be worth it even if the pay is less.

Negative environment. Consequences from a negative environment can change your personality, affect your spiritual life, and even alter your health. If it is not a positive experience in your position, either change positions or follow another chariot. This kind of environment can also hurt your family relationships.

Unappreciated. Lack of appreciation is one of the most discouraging things to subordinates that give their all to the lead person. On the other hand, when you are appreciated, not only do you stay, but you go the extra mile to please. Appreciation ranks high in a measure of components necessary for job satisfaction. It is what we all thrive on. This way we are getting our glory in a different way. Though we are not in the limelight of number one, we still get to shine. It is a simple as hearing the top guy say, "You did great!" Or to hear your peers saying, "Way to go!" It also comes when people ask for and follow your advice, then become successful and thank you for your help on their journey.

Lack of recognition. It doesn't take much for leadership to recognize subordinates who do well. Be it pride or selfishness at the first-chariot level, the lack of recognition of dedicated colleagues causes much turnover and the loss of valuable human resources. One of the admistrators at our office came up with a way to recognize individuals who go above and beyond the call of duty to help others. It is called the "Team Player Award." It is a simple card that all employees receive to pass out to that person that helped them out in an unexpected and selfless way. When an employee receives three cards from his or her peers, it is turned in and she receives a ten-dollar gift certificate from a local restaurant. It works as a constant source of recognition for jobs well done.

> ❯ *Leadership insight:* Good leadership multiplies the
>   joy and reward of success. Bad leadership multiplies

disappointment and regret even in the light of apparent success.

> *Management insight:* Establish a reward system to acknowledge people who are overlooked but deserve recognition. This shows people that their efforts aren't in vain, that others appreciate what they have accomplished, whether large or small. Failing to do so could cause major turnover.

> *Relational insight:* No one who lies to or manipulates his followers is worthy of leadership or friendship.

9

Surviving the Role
of a Subordinate Leader

Subordinates are the foundational stones of successful
enterprises.

—AUTHOR

EVEN IF YOU have all the qualifications of a good number
two, understand and possess the personal qualities, and
match the personality profile, when you get in the game, it
could be difficult. Acceptance may come slowly because you
are new. Suspicion can run high because even your friends
may not trust your motives, and breaking into the information loop may be a nightmare, but you are in the game to
play... and survive.

When leaders come from the subordinate positions, they arise
from within the group to share knowledge and skills needed for
the success of the enterprise. They participate in a leadership
team as the group moves through work stages: defining the situation and getting people to the table, visioning, planning, and
supporting the work. This activity brings you in contact with
the top leaders... in a position to influence them.

The journey to the second-chariot role requires that we all serve in subordinate roles. Somewhere along the way, we are thrust into a position where we do not have experience. With new responsibilities and no experience, what do we do to survive? Below are tips I have gleaned over the years from many different sources and personal experience that I believe will give you confidence working the number-two position:

> *Ask plenty of the right questions.* Be sure that you and your superior(s) are on the same wavelength. You must determine where they want to go and how they expect to get there.

> *Identify key players.* Other individuals, departments, and outside persons that may impact your success—your success may very well depend on their participation.

> *Be a team player.* Discuss expectations and get feedback from all those contributing, and recognize each one's accomplishments.

> *Communicate.* Use everything at your disposal to keep informed and to inform others. Don't assume that everyone is on the same page—most of the time they are not. One quick way to alienate people is to make them think that they have been excluded from important information.

> *Measurability.* Develop a system to measure your effectiveness. Get feedback from your team members, and review your goals and problem-solving efforts.

> *Report progress.* Let everyone know how it's going, especially the boss and those whom your actions affect. This will keep them on the team.

> *Learn the language each person speaks.* This does

not refer to Spanish, Japanese, German, or French. Instead, communication breakdowns occur because IT people use the language of computers, managers use the language of schedules and personnel, and administrators use the language of money. Leaders must learn to be multilingual and understand the language of each department.

> *Avoid criticizing the existing structure and processes when proposing new ideas.* Often, the people who make the decisions concerning new structure are the same employees who created the existing structure. Instead of highlighting the downfalls of a current idea, describe your concept in positive terms, i.e., how it will benefit the organization by being a helpful addition to the existing plan.

> *Be a people champion.* You must reach goals and solve problems, both of which are impossible to do without possessing the heart of the people. It takes a lot of effort to keep people in the forefront of what you do. It takes going the extra mile. When you put people as your top priority, you build the strongest possible foundation for ongoing success…for everyone involved.

> *Have the meeting before the meeting.* Save yourself a lot of opposition and resistance by meeting with key players in areas where critical decisions need to be made before the main meeting takes place. No one likes surprises that are going to affect their position or change their duties without first giving input into the decision-making process. Therefore, meet with anyone and everyone who is affected by your ideas or proposed changes before you proceed with the new idea in a leadership meeting. You will find that most of your ideas will be shot down by those affected by it if they are not consulted first.

❯ *Approach new ideas indirectly and incrementally.* Be subtle when proposing or implementing an idea. If possible, make small incremental changes to structure and strategy. If the proposed idea does not require an enormous change, you will be less likely to be met with a negative response. Learn to limit change to 20 percent of the structure at a time.

STRATEGIES FOR SUCCESS

Learn to sell your ideas upward.

The vision for the company is usually set by senior management, yet many of the best ideas and strategic change come from people in the middle or lower echelons. Use methods and tools that are effective for number twos to sell their vision upward and laterally.

People at the top can't know everything. They can't be the ones who have all the details for setting new vision and strategy—they are dependent on people below. The people in the second, third, and fourth positions are in close contact with daily operations and know the success path of the plan. They are the ones who have the information. So if you're in the middle position, you are needed by people at the top. You have to be able to tell them when things aren't going right and how to fix them. You should have vision for your own position. It has to be compatible with the vision for the whole organization, but you must communicate to the top what it is you do that's special and exciting.

How do you sell your ideas upward? The same way you sell anything: put it in terms that the other person cares about. So if you have ideas you want your boss to hear, you need to think about what he worries and cares about—his win. Tie your ideas to the existing strategy, and show how they can help reach the organization's goals. If you tie your ideas and comments to what the people at the top care about, they're going to listen. That's how all influence works.

Learn how to influence those above you. Many subordinate leaders have ideas for improvements and new strategy but lack the authority to implement these ideas. The key for subordinates to influence upward and laterally to promote an idea and gain support is to bring as many others on board with the idea as possible. When you make it "our" idea, someone in the group will have influence with the leadership. The key to all influence, whether you are at the middle, the bottom, or even at the top, is that people work on the basis of shared rewards and recognition. That is, people let themselves be influenced because they think they are going to get something they care about in return for what you're asking them to do. So if a subordinate wants to influence his or her boss, or the top management group, or peers who control strategy and resources, then figure out what each one values and give it to them. You are making deposits in their values bank and gaining their approval. These things they value are their currencies.

What currencies do they value? If you are trying to sell an idea to any leader, you can tell what he values by the kinds of things he talks about. If he cares about growth, flexibility, price, or market issues, he will always be talking about them. And so you would want to frame your arguments in terms of the things he cares passionately about. Another leader might care about long-term stability of an organization, or about creating a more humane environment for people to work in, or about being influential in the community, or more about being cutting edge in technology. Whatever it is, you need to frame your arguments in terms of things that they care about.

Similarly, with colleagues it helps to know how they are measured and rewarded, what their bosses care about, or the way in which they can shine in the organization. It also helps to know what they talk about so you can influence a peer. In this way you think about how you can help the peer accomplish his or her objective. Always give people something they care about.

Build supporting relationships and allies through relationships.

It has been my experience that building strong relationships with staff is a key in leading from a subordinate role.

First of all, you should be making relationships and connecting to people long before you know what you need from them. It is not sincere to get "friendly" just because you need someone—it's just not genuine. Subordinates who acquire influence are people who have a vast and wide network in the organization. They have friends everywhere. You will find that when you're in the habit of thinking about what matters to other people, you make connections much more quickly. That's a habit of mind, the notion that I need to tune in early and figure out what people are like, what they are all about, and find a way to make a connection to that. To do this you must take a genuine interest in them.

Often subordinate leaders come to me to rehearse all that they're doing. They share not only their successes but also their struggles and concerns. In cases like this, you need to respond by being genuinely interested in them and not about what you're going to get out of it. Rather, focus on what they're concerned about. You will soon be seen as somebody worth talking to. This is a valuable image. To ignore people until you need them alienates them. They will figure out that the only reason you are so kind all of a sudden is that you need their services.

We live in a world where people recycle through our lives, and we need to have many more connections than we know we're going to use. But these connections must be authentic on your part. It's worth doing even if it turns out that you never need their services, because you will get a reputation as someone who cares about people, who is easy to talk to, who knows how to connect, who isn't just peddling your own stuff all the time, and who isn't totally self-absorbed. And if you have that reputation, people will be drawn to you.

Reward all the players in an undertaking.

Rarely does a subordinate leader develop and implement an idea without significant assistance from others. Share benefits and reward allies and supporters. Nothing really gets done in organizations without involving a lot of people. Very seldom does one person make great decisions and carry out all the tasks alone. So it's inherent in the nature of organizations that other people are going to be involved.

There is very good research evidence that people who are effective in getting things done always share the credit. In fact, they are very generous about giving other people credit. There is no need to worry that if you give other people credit someone will say you haven't done anything. The ones you reward and give the credit to will make it known that you contributed leadership.

There are lots of ways to pay people. You can pay in recognition. You can pay in visibility. You can pay in appreciation. You should never act as if you are an island and did it all alone. It just isn't possible to get it done alone. So you need to share credit.

Make sure everyone feels like their performance was acknowledged, and play it up in a big way. Don't talk for two hours about how much you have accomplished and then say as a side note, "Oh, yes, the team really pitched in." That isn't very persuasive. You have to really mean it when you say it, and you have to be convincing because you do mean it.

Jim Collins found out something in the research he did leading to the book *Good to Great* that most people find counterintuitive: leaders of companies that really sustain themselves over time, outperforming others, are often quite humble.[23] They were people who didn't go around claiming giant things. They were steady, giving credit to others. They stuck with their values, and they weren't about me, me, me. They were about us and doing things together. That's pretty impressive data.

Make the hard decisions. Whether you're in the second or first place, you always face hard decisions. There are lessons we can learn from beyond the business world, such as the political stage, that show how leaders decide which positions to take and how to build support around a vision.

President George W. Bush made a decision that committed the United States to war with Iraq. There was controversy around it and lots of political positioning on both sides of the decision. Though so much was at stake and the decision would cost the entire world a huge price, indecision might have been even more costly. Tony Blair said something that I thought was right on: "I don't seek unpopularity as a badge of honor, but sometimes it is the price of leadership and the cost of conviction."

These two great leaders made the decision in the light of much opposition from former close allies like France and Germany and also from our supposed new friend Russia. It seemed the world was split on the matter, but a decision had to be made—and it was.

What is so difficult about leadership is that sometimes you have to go against the majority's will. As a leader you must make difficult decisions that benefit the people or the company you serve even when it is unpopular.

Great leaders often seem not to listen. I believe it is more that they weigh the advice they are given and then let their convictions or experience tilt the scales in a direction that goes against the advice they receive. It is clear in their minds what needs to be done, and they do it. Afterward, if they are successful, people think they are wonderful. But if they fail, people will criticize them openly and behind their back.

To me, it is always better to hear an issue from several people in several positions to make sure you have the big picture...then go for it. If you are right, it is another feather in your cap; if you are wrong, you have the support of those consulted in making the decision. This helps sometimes. Be careful not to make your decision along "political lines" or popular opinion. Much of the time the decisions of the majority are wrong, especially when it concerns change.

Unlike the batting average of a pro baseball player or the percentages of games a great golfer wins, you must make a high percentage of right decisions in order to maintain credibility. When you drive ahead against the opinions of others, you'd better be right. Because if you aren't, you come across as not having your act together and you will lose the cooperation of your followers. However, if you have strong feelings that you're right, act on the basis that the decision is not just for your own benefit, but for the good of everyone. If it is successful, then you're courageous, and you're a bold, outstanding, innovative leader.

To make good decisions, it is best to get as much information as time allows. Look deeper into the issue—it could be more complicated than what is apparent. Often, the real issue or problem is covered up by a façade. Gather all the facts and know the reasons, contributing factors, and persons the decision will affect.

Count the solutions. There are more than two solutions to a problem. "My way or the highway" or "straighten up or leave" may not be the best solution. Make a list of eight or ten different solutions, and choose the best one.

Choose a course of action. Often, this will require risk. But ask yourself, "What could go wrong if we do it this way?" Gather the facts and be willing to take a risk if necessary. Being too safety-conscious will cause inaction. And you can expect that lesser problems will be caused by your solution.

Learn how to recognize opportunities to do something great for the cause. Leadership and entrepreneurship are often viewed as roles that require people to go against the grain. When you go against the grain, it has to be for the right reasons and for the right results. Never go for selfish or frivolous reasons.

Entrepreneurs have boldness. An entrepreneur can see an opportunity and the eventual benefit to the organization when others cannot. It can be very difficult for you when others just don't get it or think it is a real opportunity.

However, you cannot be blinded by excitement for doing something new or innovative. Not every innovative idea works. Most of them fail. But convictions come into play in many decisions that effective leaders make, and many times they are right. But you must be ready and willing to pay the price for wrong decisions.

The world doesn't send you a guarantee when you're trying to do something new. Yet organizations depend on people recognizing opportunity. They depend on the ability of entrepreneurial leaders to recognize opportunities when they appear.

If you are someone who has a new idea, you have to be both persistent and flexible. You should listen to people around you, but when you see something that others don't, that's the chance to make a real difference.

Although we regularly see and read about leadership from CEOs, many of those leadership decisions have been prompted by actions and ideas arising from subordinate leaders. In the 1960s, it was middle managers at IBM whose determination caused them to persist (against instructions) in developing the 360 computer, one of the most successful products in the world. And it was young, lower-level managers at Toyota who developed the ideas for electronic commerce and ardently and successfully promoted use of the Web to senior management.

This is a continual process happening at virtually every organization today. People in subordinate roles have great knowledge about emerging trends in their markets, in technologies, in customer needs, and in opportunities for process improvement within their own companies and consequently are uniquely positioned to foster change in their own firms. This has always been true, and great companies count on the contributions of informed people in the middle. In fact, great careers are made by mastering the process of leading from subordinate roles.

While there are many stories to confirm the important impact of subordinate leaders, leading from the middle sounds impossible to many people. Use your gifts, learn the lessons above, and make a difference.

Setting the course in your organization. Top-level leaders rely on employees on other levels of the organization to tell them what is working and what is not. Employees who are closest to the clients often discern new trends. In a real sense, top leadership is led by others—those in the subordinate roles. Does this happen in all organizations? Yes, and these subordinate leaders can dramatically alter a company's direction and chances for success. Every organization needs the contributions of its employees at every level. You need to leverage what you know, your firsthand feel for opportunities, and then put it into appropriate action.

Whether it is new products, better processes, different use of resources, unfilled customer needs, or just critical input into the plans and actions of top management, you have an important leadership role from wherever you are in the organization. You still need to do your job well—that's how you gain credibility—but if you just sit and wait for instructions or to be recognized and pulled out of the crowd, you will not fulfill your dreams. Use your skills to help influence the future at your firm—in doing that, you shape your own future.[24]

There are many steps of action between where decisions are made and where work gets done, and there has to be leadership at every step. The key difference is the functional distance from the level at which the organization's goals are set and where they are actually achieved. Subordinate leaders are closer to where the actual work gets done. The more practical a leader's goals, the easier they are to accomplish. First in commands are further away from the actual work both physically and functionally. Senior level leaders must focus more on things like organizational culture, values, vision, strategy, and goals. Therefore the closer to the task the action gets, the more their subordinate leaders must lead for them. It is also easier for subordinates because of the personal involvement with their followers. Some describe the differences as direct and indirect leadership.

Leading Up

People will participate in a world they help create.

—AUTHOR UNKNOWN

LEADING UP, LEADING those who are your superiors, is not a natural skill, but it can be mastered, and there are few better ways to appreciate its exercise than to study those who have had to apply it. Watching their efforts can provide lessons for leading up when it really counts. Great subordinate leaders like Vice President Dick Cheney, Colin Powell, Donald Rumsfeld, and others in the present administration are examples of how effective subordinates can be in bringing success to a cause. They are actually providing leadership for the president of the United States, not just taking orders. This becomes obvious when they say things that are not in sync with the president's latest statements on a matter. They are leading—synchronizing comes later—but at some point they must lead. In cabinet meetings they are all brought on the same page and help the president form his opinions on the matters at hand, but in the field they lead.[25]

There is room for every subordinate to be great. We can be great in our own right when we understand that what we do actually leads the top.

THE COURAGEOUS SUBORDINATE

Leading up requires fortitude and perseverance. Subordinates might fear how superiors will respond to their advance, but every person should carry the responsibility to do what he can when it will make a positive difference in the organization. He must tell a superior what he or she ought to hear. Many strategies and more than a few organizations have failed when the subordinates could see the problems but hesitated to inform leadership. This takes courage and may come across as being negative, but truth is the only thing you can build success on.

THE FULL-SERVICE SUBORDINATE

There are reasons subordinates become tentative in leading up. Some are reluctant because they just don't want the hassle. They are satisfied ruling their own world. They feel comfortable controlling their own environment even though intrusions from leadership above rattle that world from time to time. Others are hesitant because they feel the risk is not worth the reward. They led up before and either did not receive any recognition for their efforts or were criticized when it did not go well. You need to be willing to give the credit away for accomplishments and also take the heat for mistakes if you really want to be a "full-service" subordinate.

The feeling of tentativeness about leading up from some subordinates is not always their fault. Leaders at the top should encourage employees to speak up and ask for help when needed, and tell them what they need to know, to fill in for their shortcomings when success is threatened.

"Managers, no matter where they are in the organization, need to show they are open to new ideas by changing their minds, admitting they were wrong or that they didn't have enough information, and publicly acknowledging the person who helped them see the light. All of those things are very important," says Erin Fuller, vice president of education and executive director of the Research Foundation for the Community Associations Institute (CAI).[26]

When you are asked by leadership to give input to a plan or situation, give the information you have. Share insights about how it will affect others in the organization and how you think it will promote or impede the success of the vision. Be available to jump in where needed to carry out the plan.

Take Courage to Lead Up

"Unsatisfied satisfaction" is a term my pastor and mentor used to describe his quest for more in his spiritual life. Unsatisfied satisfaction says, "Yes, I have more than I had, but I am thirsty still." A common element among people who successfully lead up is a driving urge to make things happen on high, an unflinching willingness to take charge when not fully in command. Those who lead up are enemies of the status quo and are willing to risk obliterating their comfort zone for something more meaningful.

Someone is leading up. It is either those who are stubbornly resistant to change and progress or those with vision for the best possible outcome. Top-level leaders are influenced by somebody—so let it be *you*.

Subordinate leaders have specific roles to play and must fulfill their responsibilities in these roles. Some of a number two's leadership roles could be the following.

Execute Strategy and Deliver Results

Commitment is gained or lost at the grassroots level by leaders and managers of specific functions, departments, or areas. Leaders provide the tools, and managers who train need to communicate strategy and build commitment throughout the organization. Ideas are basically worthless without tangible outcomes. You need to turn them into reality. In other words, you need to execute. *Execution* is the ability to mesh strategy with reality, align people with goals, and achieve the promised results. I have been part of many great brainstorming ideas that produced no action and no results. So execution is the key, and many leaders are not very good at it. You have to align yourself as a leader/manager to be involved in the execution of a strategy as well as the decision-making process.

Understand the necessity of change. The bottom line in executing strategy is delivering results—making sure there is productivity. With output from ideas and strategic planning, you are on your way to success. But without change, you will have diminishing results. Look at this quote from Jack Dixon: "If you focus on results, you will never change. If you focus on change, you will get results."[27] Without change, you cannot keep up with the changing environment that affects supply and demand.

Motivate and inspire people to perform with excellence. You may say, "That is the job of the boss." It is the job of both effective leaders and successful managers, including the boss. You cannot lead or manage people you don't communicate to, and you can't motivate and inspire unless you communicate well. It is vitally important to be able to inspire from the implementation and execution level. And execution of ideas mainly falls to the subordinate leaders and managers.

Recognition and advancement are two of the greatest motivators in an organization. Without these factors, people are reluctant to respond to necessary changes and only give minimal effort to the job. On the flipside, however, when people are recognized for their contribution and are promoted because of performance, there will be high output.

Manage, develop, and retain key talent. There's that word *managing.* As we will explore later in this book, managing is a leader's tool to keep people in a place where they are best suited and most productive. It is a leader's task to develop key talent in an organization and keep them on board. If you, as a subordinate leader, are the reason that key players leave the company, your job can be in jeopardy. You must know how to manage talented people well and continually get their ongoing commitment to work and produce for the enterprise.

It's like recruiting great college baseball players into the minor leagues. This is where they are appraised, developed, and eventually brought on into the majors as significant contributors to the team. Who does this developing? Minor league managers do. If these players are not retained and developed, there is little chance that the major league team will ever have a winning club.

The most critical and scarce resource in today's competitive world is talented people. Finding and keeping the people needed to succeed is the biggest challenge facing business today. Despite the enormous costs associated with turnover, few companies have a comprehensive strategy to attract and retain their most valuable resource. For the most part, subordinate level leaders are given the responsibility to do this.

Build relationships and influence others. Marketing, sales, service, and repeat business are almost totally dependent on building long-term relationships with people.

The president of Olde South Candles related this story to me. A salesperson was responsible for a major client but was not performing well in areas of new business and maintenance of smaller accounts. But this salesperson took good care of the large client and had developed a long-term relationship with the key people there. When a discussion came up about the possibility of replacing the salesperson, the client responded, "No way; we want to keep this person." It was clear that the relationship was more important to them than the salesperson's performance.

In business, you need to focus on at least three relationship areas. *Customer relationships* are those relationships that define who your product or service is for and how to please them with service and respect. If you cannot give them what they want and need, you will lose them to some other enterprise. Then there are *employee relationships*. It is critical to know that employees are not products and are not expendable, but are very critical to the success of the enterprise. Many employees are treated like necessary appendages and little more than a means to an end. In the long term, this produces disloyalty among the employees, who begin to cost the company lost revenues due to sick leave, theft, laziness, and other bad work habits. Employees must be seen as valuable partners and made to feel like they are the major reason that your company is successful.

The term *community relations* can be boiled down to knowing that community is bigger than the products it consumes and needs to be respected and served in the process of doing business. Wise leaders always keep their finger on the pulse of what is happening in their community, whether it is the local people, customer base, or industry community. They understand how to communicate to that community.

BUILDING EFFECTIVE TEAMS

The key to successful implementation of process, production, maintenance, and improvement lies in building of participatory, multifunctional, and multidisciplinary teams. These teams can be permanent, or they can be created on a more temporary basis for solving specific problems. The team will play a central role in planning and implementing initiatives taken on by the company. It has been said, "People will participate in a world they help create."

Once formed, the team needs to be trained in concepts and techniques for problem solving and focusing on the end users of the product or service. We will cover more on team building in part two of this book "The Successful Subordinate Manager." Suffice it to say, you will need the ability to build effective teams and to solve problems as a team leader.

PART II

THE SUCCESSFUL
SUBORDINATE MANAGER

Sarah Jenkins had outperformed her peers for years and was promoted up the ladder of her company to the sales manager job. This position included not only overlooking the sales force, but also managing the day-to-day affairs of customer care, shipping and receiving, and keeping accounts receivables up to date, not to mention product quality and handling complaints. Her new position was so unfamiliar to her that she appeared at a complete loss about what to do most of the time.

Sarah had proven that she was a self-starter and a motivator as a team member, but now as a manager she seemed inept. How would she make sure that every task was covered, every employee was doing what he or she was gifted to do, and everyone was always on the same page? She needed help, but where would the help come from?

Everyone manages something. So the question is not whether we are managers, but whether we are *good* or *bad* managers. Sometime in life you will be called on to manage money, paperwork, people's time and tasks, and maybe even chaos. So get ready to manage something. Leaders that fail at management are not good leaders.

11

Total Area Management

FIRST OF ALL, it is necessary to understand what we are normally given to manage. In many cases, we are given "things" to manage. "Take this leadership material and start a training program" or "Make sure we stay on course to finish this job before the deadline." This seems simple. However, nearly everything we are given to do requires the involvement of people. So the more we know about leading people, the easier it is going to be to manage things that are given to us.

Total area management is in goals, teams, and individuals. Each aspect must be managed properly in order to get the desired results.

Goals are your objectives and the tasks required to meet those objectives. In other words, we set goals with the results in mind, identify the tasks that will give us those results, and solve the problems that we have to solve in order to do the tasks and reach our goals.

It is necessary, then, to manage the people that perform the tasks, i.e., communicate the task, equip them to do the task, resolve any conflicts that come up during time the task is being done, and then ensure quality control in order to get the final result you planned for. Of course, you must do all of this within the prescribed budget.

Since your job will involve people, you need to find people. This is the team-building aspect of total area management. If the job can be done by you alone, then there is nothing to manage but your own time and perhaps a budget. If it requires a team, people with differing skills and expertise, then you must recruit, build, motivate, and maintain a strong, unified team. When you have done this, you have the potential to do just about anything. Nothing is impossible if you can get the right people to work together.

Once you have the team together, you will see and understand the need to develop each individual on that team. This may require only that you encourage them separately and recognize each one's contribution to the effort. Or it may go as far as seeing that each one receives specialized training to perform effectively. Whatever it takes to get the team functioning productively, you or someone else will have to do individually to some extent. When individuals work as a team, they will be more productive than if they worked separately. Give attention to individual needs.

The Makeup of the Enterprise

Let's look at your business or the enterprise you work for.

Corporation—Community—Cause

Every growing enterprise can be defined with these three terms: *corporation*, *community*, and *cause*. Whether it's a pharmaceutical, a toymaker, a nonprofit, or a grocery store, you must envision and understand these three aspects of it.

Corporation. A corporation is a group authorized to act as an individual. They deal with all the aspects of community in the area of housing the corporation, financing the business, planning, and organization.

In order to be a successful "corporate" manager, you must understand how to deal with things like bylaws, administration, schedules, and the like. Budgets, staff, job descriptions, partners, buildings, and organizational charts all work together to make up the corporation. These are all corporate issues.

Without expertise in these areas, a subordinate manager can make major errors in judgment and cause serious harm to the enterprise. It is very important that every individual who has the role of leading a department or is responsible for corporate transactions has training in the issues of managing the resources and structure of that corporation.

Community. Think of the community of employees, customers, wholesalers, bankers, and family that make up your company. This is your community. Every business, church, or civic organization contains community, and we must learn how to exist in harmony within that community to be successful.

You often hear of corporations that develop a strong sense of community within their business structure. Mary Kay Cosmetics comes to mind. The leadership at Mary Kay has created a great sense of belonging and camaraderie—from pink automobiles to great motivational rallies, all for the family of women who want to make something of their lives. Even large conglomerates become a family of companies. For example, General Electric manufactures and sells everything from jet engines for military helicopters to ice-cream makers—this is the GE family.

Then there's the church family, the civic club, the alumni from the university...the list goes on. Our world is made up of unlimited number of communities.

Where people communicate, community is formed. Communication is one of if not the most important thing you do in your company, whether you are selling candles or building a community church. Communication is vital.

"Peter Drucker, often called the 'father of American management,' claims that 60 percent of all management problems are a result of faulty communication. A leading marriage counselor says that at least half of all divorces result from faulty communication between spouses. And criminologists tell us that upwards of 90 percent of all criminals have difficulty communicating with other people."[28]

In the Management 2 class that I took at LSU back in the early nineties, communication was described as having two levels: the words and the music. The words are what we say, and the music is how we say it. When communications are congruent, the words and music convey the same meaning or feeling—they go together. *Congruence* means to flow with. When communications are incongruent, there is a disparity between the person's word and music. They come across insincere or dishonest.

In a crisis situation, the opportunity exists to make friends or enemies, depending on the words/music levels or balance. If the words and music convey a positive "I care" message, you can build a better relationship. If the words and music convey a negative, insincere, or abrasive unconcern for the welfare of the person, the message will create a very dedicated enemy. It is easy to destroy trust and camaraderie with the wrong choice of words and music.

Wherever people gather for a common cause or interest, there is community. Have you ever gone by a place where a hole was being dug and seen a group of men standing around? Maybe a better question is, have you ever gone by a place where a hole was being dug that you *haven't* seen a group of men standing around?

I always thought it strange that men gather around anytime they see a hole being dug. I figured they wanted to help the guy with the shovel, but NOT SO! If you pay attention the next time you pass by a crowd at a hole digging, you'll only see one guy doing the work. The others are just standing around discussing the hole or something else.

Hole digging spans the gap between rich and poor, between white collar and blue. It spans any and all distinguishable traits. And that is how community works. No matter what we are doing, we like having others around...just to be there. We *need* community.

Cause. Your cause is the values-based reason why your enterprise exists. It is the passion element of what you do, the "pull out all of the stops" obsession with its success. Without a sense of cause, you would shut down the enterprise at the first obstacle that threatened the community. However, with a strong sense of cause, when adversaries come, you instead rally the community into a great army to defeat any threat against it.

A sense of cause gives everyone a belief that the good of the corporation is bigger than the corporation itself. A sense of cause believes that its purpose is greater than profit alone and gives the community the conviction that sacrifice for profitability and the survival of the enterprise is worthwhile. A sense of cause is insurance for survival.

There are so many causes that we join our hearts to, some for the fight against cancer, some for equality, some for peace and unity. One such cause was embraced by mothers of some professional basketball players. They got together to record a CD for the cause of peace. "It is my hope and prayer that this music CD will inspire people to come together in unity. And may it also send a message that we need to continue to love one another and create peace in the world," said one of the mothers.

The "cause" brought people together from all over the country to do something they thought was important—promoting peace.

When you neglect the "cause" metaphor, you risk losing the emotional connection people have with the enterprise.

Make sure you communicate the "why" of your existence to your staff and customers—it will go a long way in keeping them on board.

Corporate aspects neglected: Money, buildings, organization charts, job descriptions, planning, management.

Problems: After time, you can't house the community without a building or office structure. (If you don't put money into a building, you won't have a place to build "people.") You can't fund the cause without cash. There must be organization and process, management and support. Community and cause suffer without corporation. Energy and passion exist, but work is chaotic, and energy is dissipated through ineffective and inefficient allocation of resources. Factors increase exponentially as the business grows. New businesses and growing churches face this challenge daily.

Community untended: Coldness and sterility, unloving, lacks compassion.

Many entrepreneurial organizations have cause and corporation, yet lose sight of community. People have only utilitarian value. People exist as a means to an end, not as ends in themselves.

Cause is left untended: When we forget "why" we exist and the bigger picture of our contribution to society, we will lose positive movement.

The result is that the enterprise begins to lack momentum and energy because the workforce doesn't see anything bigger than itself and becomes ingrown, introspective. The result is people looking out for themselves and becoming territorial and possessive of position and things. It eventually implodes.

12

Finding Value in What You Do

THERE HAS TO be value in all aspects of working in an organization in order to keep the organization and its employees moving forward. A paycheck is not enough to capture the imagination and excitement of the personnel. "Payday" must come in different forms. As a matter of fact, it is well known that money is not the number one reason people work where they work. As a subordinate manager, it can be difficult to overcome negativism and passivity from upper management, but set your sights on bringing value to your team by showing them value in multiple ways. This chart reveals some ways to show value.

Value In	Value In	Value From
Doing the task itself	Accomplishing the task	Reward, motivation, recognition
Working with others	The end of the product	The greater sense of cause
Corporate family	Fulfillment in results	Being part of the success story

When people see value in all aspects of what they do, they do it better, longer, with more accuracy, and with a better attitude, which makes everyone more successful.

It only comes true in fairy tales.

Cinderella, abused and forgotten, through no actions of her own, finds Prince Charming and marries into fortune and a life of leisure and bliss. She lives happily ever after. This is the "Cinderella Syndrome" that is fixed in the minds of so many people in the workforce. They are sure that *one day* their Prince Charming or their proverbial ship will come in and sweep them into the front office, where they will rule. This of course almost never happens. Action precedes achievement and accomplishment. We must consistently be doing the right things with the right attitude and motive to build a success-filled life story.

Law of Positive Action: "None of the secrets of success will work...until you do."

We should underline the word *positive* here. The potential we have for success will not be realized in one year, or even ten years, but over a lifetime. Consider this, how do you measure your cumulative experience? Do you have thirty years experience or one years experience thirty times? It is better to wear an old, scuffed wedding ring than a new one each year. An example of this is that investing in the stock market has historically paid good dividends when investments are made in small amounts, consistently, over a long period of time. Our efforts will pay dividends in the same scenario, not by starting and stopping a hundred times, but by sowing systematically in the field we want someday to harvest. Consistent positive actions will bring us the expected results in time.

We judge ourselves by *our potential*; others judge us by *our performance*. We certainly must discover our potential and work to reach it; however, we will never become effective until we see ourselves in the light of our *performance*. To expect others to see our potential is not always reasonable, so perform. The closer we move to ideal performance, the happier we will be. There is an ideal, and we should be in a never-ending quest to be as effective as possible. This requires that we always be learners. Never stop improving on who you are and what you do. Being in a subordinate position does not limit your potential. This type of subordinate leader is one who influences the boss's decisions the most.

Subordinate "Leader/Manager"

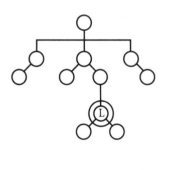

Influences Boss with:
> Honesty
> Integrity
> Character
> Hard work

Accomplishment:
> Creativity
> Loyalty
> Dependability

Subordinates must learn the goals of the company and specifically of the boss, and they must work to assure the boss's *success*.

You will experience failure along the way and will see reasons why you failed. But solutions must accompany reasons for failure. Denying inevitable failure is not the solution either. It is your job to help the boss succeed and to protect him from failure when at all possible. It is vital to realize when a project will fail without corrective action. Do not let the boss get blindsided by a failed project that you knew in advance was doomed.

Happiness comes with success, problem solving, reaching goals, and recognition for doing a good job. In each of us is a sense of our potential for success and how we should strive to reach that potential. The closer we come to fulfilling that sense of potential, the happier we are.

Below is a "Happiness Scale." Draw one for yourself, and try to determine where you are in reaching your true potential.

Happiness Scale

The Need for Success in Our Life—Happiness
The Need for Action in Our Life—Accomplishment

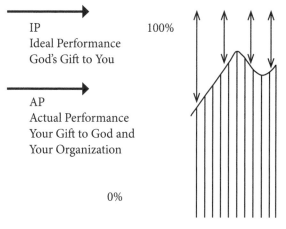

IP
Ideal Performance
God's Gift to You

100%

AP
Actual Performance
Your Gift to God and
Your Organization

0%

The closer our actual performance is to ideal performance, the happier and more successful we are.

Note:
A. We judge ourselves by our potential.
　　1. Intentions

B. Others judge us by our performance.
　　1. Accomplishments

13

Recruiting Help

IF YOU ARE going to accomplish any worthwhile task, you will need to involve people. Learning recruiting skills is a mandatory undertaking. Recruiting is a lost art in most arenas, whether in profit or nonprofit businesses, but it can be critical to the success of any enterprise.

Webster's defines *recruit* as "to replenish; restore or increase the health, vigor, or intensity of." This is like refilling your oxygen tank in your scuba gear, or bringing fresh athletes off the bench—it is absolutely the difference between winning and losing. The same is true in business. We must revitalize our business teams with new recruits, volunteers, and rotating members —whatever it takes to keep the players on the field fresh.

Be clear about your vision—make it clear so that people who hear it can run with it. Be sure about it yourself—be convinced. Be excited about it. Enthusiasm is contagious, so inspire people with clear, enthusiastic communication about the vision of your enterprise. Don't expect them to get excited if you aren't. When your vision is unclear, you force others to define what they think the vision is, and confusion results.

Recruit people who have a reputation for working hard and possessing skill. Throughout the world, there is a demand for skilled, super-skilled, and supra-skilled people. To find a *meister* in your field is a tough job. Headhunters get enormous fees for their skills in recruiting and for their database of highly skilled job candidates. This tough job must be done. But be careful that the person you recruit into your office is a person who has good standing with his or her peers and in the community at large. Negative character traits in a new recruit negate his skill competencies. Choose those whom you respect. Respect those whom you choose. Once you find the right people, respect them as individuals and as skilled workers, and let them function in their gifting. Nothing is more humiliating than to be recruited to do an important job only to be relegated to some minor status position to languish. Assure the recruits that they will not be working alone. They need to know that you work as a team, that it is an effort by everyone. The team concept means we succeed by helping each other. The success of each individual ensures the success of the team. Reassure them that you will train them where they lack expertise, and then do it.

People like to know what the rewards are for their participation in anything. However, most rewards need not be monetary to be attractive. Recognition, showing appreciation, and a sense of purpose and significance are often more important to people than monetary rewards.

Before you allow people on the team, let them get an inner confirmation that they should be part of the team. If it is confirmed in their heart, they will endure hardships. They need to be sure that it is what is best for them. Then encourage the new recruits to take an active part in the initiatives of the company.

Show them how action brings results and results end up in recognition and eventually promotion and financial reward.

When building teams and recruiting a leader, make sure that the lead horse is strong enough to pull the wagon. Often your recruits will need training in order to lead others. Give it to them. Remember, though, to choose the right people. Do that, and right things will happen; choose the wrong people, and wrong things will happen.

Continue recruiting to offset turnover. There is a constant need to recruit new people for growing companies and increasing numbers of projects. Recruiting brings in excited and enthusiastic new people.

Leadership is the people side of management. You *lead* people; you *manage* things. And because people need a sense of direction (vision) and of belonging to the effort (being part of something significant), strong leadership must be in place. Everyone needs to accomplish goals in their life in order to feel successful, and they need to know how they are performing, good or bad. We all need the support of our leaders to help us succeed, and we all need to work to be successful as individuals.

> The strength of the pack is in the wolf; the strength of the wolf is in the pack.[29]
>
> —RUDYARD KIPLING

Getting Others to Participate

IN ORDER TO get people to want to participate in what you are doing, you have to take them through a "buy in" process. Many of my struggles in trying to lead people as a second-in-command leader/manager originated with the issue of ownership. Remember, people will participate in a world they help create.

On one occasion, I had worked on a project that was to be the answer-all solution to our tracking of leadership. I worked for months to come up with this great piece of work. When it was all said and done, only 20 percent of our leaders would use it. It worked for the 20 percent, and it worked for me, but the others would not use it. What was the problem? They had no sense of ownership. Had they been in on the process of creating this tracking manual, it would have been just what the doctor ordered. But the lack of ownership on their part made my "fabulous" work useless to them.

Some valuable lessons were learned through this experience. When you have an assignment from the boss to create something that will be used by others in the organization, try to bring in everyone that the decision or creation will affect for their input. What does this do? It gives them ownership. Not only do you get better cooperation when it is time to implement the new idea, but also it is a better idea because of their input.

This is how to approach the process now. Let those whom the project or idea will affect be in on the decision-making process. If they help make the decision, they will commit. If they help make the decision to do it, it's partly their idea, and that means they are part owners. Encourage each one to make suggestions. When they make suggestions, try to develop those suggestions. When you develop their suggestions, it reveals whether or not the plan is good. If the plan is good, try it to see if it works. If is doesn't work, everyone will see and know that you need more and better ideas.

As team members come up with new plans, allow them to test their plans. When they are allowed to test their plans, they gain insights on how they work to satisfy the objective. If they don't test their plans, they will never know if they work or not. And if they aren't allowed to try their own plans, they might not give yours a chance either. Give them the opportunity to perfect or eliminate their idea. If it proves to be a good plan, then you have something to work with. If the plan doesn't work, you will both know its weaknesses.

When you go through a process like this, you have the chance to discover the creative ideas of your team members and to arrive at a workable plan *together*. Participation nurtures commitment. When you find the right plan together, you'll have your employees' commitment to do it. The goal of the team is to find that workable plan.

Once a workable plan is accepted, then you can work together on the success of the plan. When success is obtained, there is great motivation to continue with a high level of commitment.

Some other guidelines for individual participation. Never put a team member in a position where he is totally responsible to win. Don't give him the impression that "If this doesn't work, it will be your fault." Instead of putting pressure on the one individual, make every suggestion a "group idea." "It was suggested that we..." Do not attach the idea to the person too closely.

Do not "overpraise" one idea before hearing the others. You can squelch the participation of the others by doing this. However, when an idea is adopted and it works, spread it around. You need everyone's input, because people are the only resource you have that can innovate.

Celebrate the success of the plan, and give recognition where due. The acknowledgment of success and rewarding a job well done are great motivation to do it again. Accomplishment brings much satisfaction.

Now enact the plan again, and recruit new helpers. A successful venture will ensure continued commitment and many new recruits. You can now build a reserve of committed people to carry out the plan indefinitely.

In situations where you are leading a creative team, try to avoid dictating to people. Dictators are the least productive people on earth. Study the dictators of the world. First, they exert control and use intimidation to exploit people, and they constantly fear retribution. Under these circumstances, people check out emotionally and rebellion builds in their hearts. Eventually there is a coup and the dictator is overthrown.

If you constantly dictate to people, they will lose initiative and wait around for you to tell them what to do. Use statements like, "I need your input. Can you give me some ideas?" And "What do you think will work?" Encourage discussion, and listen to their answers.

It is important to understand that when you teach people

how to make decisions for themselves, you teach them to become leaders. If you always make decisions for them, they will always only be able to follow. Ultimately you have to get the work done through people. What God has called you to do you cannot accomplish alone. Involving people ensures longevity. It will outlast your personal involvement.

Delegation

THERE ARE MANY reasons to delegate responsibilities to others. Without delegation, you are too involved in other areas of lesser priority that keep you from doing your job effectively. The big job gets neglected, and you miss important deadlines while working on more trivial matters. You have trained employees who could help balance the workload—you need the help, and they need the challenge. Besides, have you ever considered that someone else might do a better job than you? We don't delegate to get out of necessary work but to allow us to do the work that is most necessary.

When discerning the right (best) person to delegate important responsibilities to, look for certain qualities. This person must share your vision and be a determined follower. She must also be equipped to take on the responsibility. A main issue in delegating for success is to make sure the person to whom the responsibility is delegated is capable and trainable.

For continued success, that person must desire to see the greater success and improved production. In other words, she must have a success mentality. This requires that she is willing to stay under authority and accept the oversight and counsel of the ones who are ultimately accountable. Anybody might volunteer, but only a few will be reliable enough to accept important responsibilities and follow through with them to success.

DELEGATION GUIDELINES

Delegate authority and responsibility to the lowest possible level. This is effective because the person performing the job has the most knowledge about that specific job. Get the best people you can find (recruit); get agreement on objectives (gain commitment); then turn them loose to do their jobs (delegate). A time must come when you just let go and let others do the job that needs to be done.

Have confidence in your people, and have the courage to stand back and let them make mistakes.

We are finite and must realize that growth requires sharing the workload to get everything done. And wouldn't it be depressing to be assigned only tasks that you could do alone? A key function of delegation is to *develop people* under your supervision, not just get rid of work. Without new developing talent in the human resources pipeline, the organization will lose the competency factor. You should always raise the level of competency in the organization, or you will soon begin to lose quality in your product and service to your customers.

Delegation is one of our most powerful tools for reproducing skills in others.

The success of your business ultimately depends on how you develop *people,* not processes. People make processes work. They make structures effective, and people, not business plans, reach goals. Select people not only for the sake of the task, but also for the development of the person. There may be people in your organization who will rise up to become important assets to the company with a little training and delegation of responsibilities.

As a person is in the process of accomplishing the delegated responsibilities, you should supervise him or her and provide ongoing support, encouragement, and training. Good supervision is the act of getting average people to do superior work. Develop greatness in these people through delegation.

Avoid reverse delegation.

Reverse delegation is when the delegate gives the task back to you. After you have delegated responsibility, your delegate may come and want you to take the task back because of problems. Help her grow by requiring her to solve the problems herself and follow through with her commitment. Encourage people to find their own solutions to problems and make decisions themselves. You are there for counsel, not to make all the decisions. They need the opportunity to grow and develop, so keep the ball in their court. Give people the chance to conquer new worlds of responsibility. They will grow, and you will end up with more capable helpers.

There are certain inherent hindrances to delegation that are common to every manager. These hindrances come from an old paradigm we picked up from the generation of managers and leaders before us.

1. You must have it done your *way.* This attitude comes from insecurity and a superiority complex that was formed when you worked for people who gave you no room for error. It also stems from a pride issue, where you always wanted people to see how good you were at what you do.

2. You don't trust other people to do it well enough. This is somewhat like the issue above but includes the lack of trust in those you work with. This attitude is held by those of us who have been let down by others' lack of ability. Instead of training those around you to excel, you complain about their ineptness.

3. *You are unstable in your position, thinking that you may be outshined.* This attitude is prevalent because, on many occasions in our lives, we have been robbed of the credit for great things we have done. Someone else either stole the credit, or the accomplishment went unnoticed and was never rewarded. Remember, however, that if your subordinates shine brightly enough, they will reflect on you!

4. *You don't see the big picture, failing to recognize that you cannot accomplish everything alone.* I would feel slighted if the only responsibility delegated to me could be accomplished by me alone. The big picture will always include many people working together to accomplish a meaningful goal. Gaze beyond your own abilities and see what the potential end result could look like.

Management Mentalities

MENTALITIES AND ATTITUDES develop in the workplace because of how we are treated, how we are recognized for what we do, or for not sensing purpose or a future with the organization that we work for. It is our job to help develop the right mentality in the minds of our staff and workers.

The *job mentality* is primarily concerned with performing current duties with little thought to what the benefit to the enterprise should be. An "I just work here" attitude develops and contributes to a lack of concern for the other vital aspects of the work. The end result is isolation from the team and loss of the real and original vision. You become engaged in the work but not in the purpose.

The *control mentality* is concerned with the function of all aspects of the enterprise: the government, authority, and decisions. *Control* is the key word to ensure that a proper form of government and work style are perpetuated and that there is adherence to the standard.

The end result is that accomplishment is often sacrificed on the altar of "doing it right" or "doing it like it has always been done" regardless of the goal. Many control-type dogmas take the place of fresh directions that need to be a part of the plan in order to keep up with changing circumstances. The organization becomes bogged down in an organizational rut.

The *goal mentality* is the right mentality in my opinion. There is nothing magical about setting goals and working toward those goals until you complete them—it is very logical. Simply setting goals does not guarantee success any more than planning to catch some fish produces fish. Purpose and right actions must take place in the right environment for success to happen. But you also have goals to know why and for what you are working for.

The goal mentality says that government, authority, decisions, procedures, jobs, and controls must serve a specific purpose in reaching the goal established and must accomplish all objectives in the process. The "Law of Positive Action" ensures that the goal will be reached. Controls are built in, but the goal is not sacrificed on the altar of doing it right. By measuring all actions with the goal mentality, you will save time, accomplish more, and not waste human resources.

Problem solving—make problem solving your number one goal. You can have great goals, but without solving the problems that prevent those goals from being met, you will get nowhere. To solve problems consistently, ask yourself a few questions: "Have I seen a similar problem before?" "What do I know about this kind of problem?" "How did I solve it the last time?" Then, set out on a strategy to solve the problem, keeping notes of what went wrong to cause the problem and how it was corrected.

There are four kinds of people in the world. People *who watch* things happen, people *to whom* things happen, people who *do not know what* is happening, and people *who make* things happen. It is people with a goal mentality who keep organizations alive and thriving. Only 25 percent of employees say they do their best all the time; 75 percent admit they could be more effective than they are at the moment; and 50 percent say they only do as much as is required. And a higher percentage of people each year feel less secure in their position or job. This all works to create the "job" mentality. When there is a job mentality, people aren't motivated to do better, and personal quality and integrity wane. You must keep a goal mentality to maintain the drive and commitment necessary to become successful.

Time Management

HAVE YOU EVER asked yourself, "Why do some people seem to accomplish significant things and still have 'free time' available, while others of us seem constantly pressured by time and complete very little that's important?" What is the difference between these kinds of people? The difference is how well we understand and use the precious resource of time.

Time can be defined as a series of events. Albert Einstein said, "Time has no independent existence apart from the order of events by which we measure it."[30] Webster's dictionary defines *time* as "a continuum in which events succeed one another from past through present to future."

In the light of these definitions, we can say that time management is *event control,* gaining control of events in our life that both exhaust us and strengthen us, helping us to achieve our highest priorities.

Two different types of events take place daily: *events within our control* and *events beyond* our control. When we control events in our lives, we are more productive and experience less stress related to our job and life. If we allow ourselves to be controlled by influences around us and beyond our control, we lose grip on our lives and stress begins to take its toll.

The way to maintain control of events in our lives is to create a plan and do all that is within our power to live by it. Planning is the key to event control. Planning is predetermining future events and seeing to it that they happen. To succeed in our planning, we must be at peace with ourselves, with others, and with God. Otherwise every unplanned event that intersects our lives will upset our cart and our plan with it.

Why should we plan? Someone said, "Time is a daily treasure that attracts many robbers." This is so true. Think of the daily distractions in your life: phone calls, interruptions at your desk, traffic delays, people who "need" to talk to you...the list goes on. Decisions have to be made daily as to who will control your time. It is up for grabs, so you'd better catch it before someone else does.

There are many reasons why we don't plan. Primarily we don't plan because we don't know how. But there are simple and effective ways to plan that will give the control of the events in your life back to you.

First of all, find a place that is relatively free of distractions where you can create your plan. Review your long-range objectives often, and break down large goals into controllable events. Make sure the number of tasks and the amount of time required for each is well within the time available in your day. Then set specific daily goals while you anticipate obstacles. Then make a "to do" list and follow it religiously.

Prioritize your tasks by delineating them as *vital, important,* and those that *can be done later* or *be delegated.*

Deal with time robbers. Develop the "pit stop" mentality. When one thing is completed, get started on the next item on your agenda. Don't wait around. When a car enters the pit stop during a NASCAR race, the team is equipped with its tools, knows its functions, and is ready to work. They jump on the car, perform all the tasks, and complete repairs in twenty seconds. This should be your attitude. Don't sit around and reward yourself every time you complete the smallest task. You will never get anything done.

The "pit stop" mentality demands that you control procrastination, interruptions, clutter, and useless meetings, and it may require delegation and working through others.

18

Team Building

W HAT DO YOU look for in potential leaders? I have identified three qualities that must be present in order to get
effective team players. I call them "Triple-A Players." Triple-A
players are *available,* they must have time and be willing to
give that time to your cause. They must have a good *attitude;*
they must have a servant's attitude that is cooperative and positive. And they can *afford* to be on the team. These players must
be able to afford to give time, money, and emotional energy to
the task at hand.

If people aren't available when you need them, you cannot
use them. Many people mean well when they volunteer...only
to fall out when asked to make the commitment. People with
negative attitudes will have to be dragged everywhere you
want to take the team. It is not worth it to bring negative people along. And people who are in debt and have to work all the

time, or are focused on the financial aspect of their commitment, will never be able to keep up with the team. This goes for those who do not have the time or emotional margin in their lives to give extra to the cause. When family problems or other personal problems overwhelm people, they will not be able to go the extra mile for the enterprise.

To many, team building is the difficult chore of getting reluctant people to join you in an exercise to which there is no real solution. To others, it is finding people you want to work with to solve problems that keep the enterprise from attaining important goals. How you perceive team building will determine whether you successful at it or not. When you pull people together to work on a project, you have to realize that you are multiplying the brainpower, creativity, energy, and ideas you will need to make the right things happen. And even though there may be participants you won't see eye to eye with, their contribution may be your success.

To build effective teams, you have to build rapport with each person in the group in order to ensure everyone's participation. Working in effective teams is essential for problem solving and completion of tasks. Build your first team when you are developing ideas. Many times, at the beginning of a project there may not be enough information. Working as a team and brainstorming the idea creates enough information to get started. Doing so continuously will keep the project on target.

A team (two or more people collaborating to reach a goal) can accomplish more than one person in most cases. There is a difference between team and committee. Webster's defines *team play* as "collective play with mutual assistance of team members; cooperative effort." A *committee* is defined as "a body of persons delegated to consider, investigate, take action, or report on some matter." A team works together to accomplish a certain task, while a committee may meet to determine if and when the task needs to be done.

The team takes on the role of leadership until each task is assigned. Then the person or group that is assigned a particular task provides the leadership needed. Teamwork increases your personal proficiency by 30 percent or more. Improve your performance with teamwork, and realize that no one person can do everything. You can be a star or have a star team.

A team must satisfy two needs: (1) action that brings desired results, and (2) the maintenance of those results.

Simple planning

1. What is the task? (Define the problem.)

2. How should we approach it? (Procedure) Choose one procedure and stick with it.

3. What criteria should be met? (Stay within boundaries.)

4. Measuring the benefits of our decision. (Is it adequate?)

5. Importance of reaching the goal.

Team synergy is an all-important ingredient for a successful finish.

Synectics is defined as "a theory or system of problem-stating and problem-solution based on creative thinking that involves free use of metaphor and analogy in informal interchange within a carefully selected small group of individuals of diverse personality and areas of specialization."

When synergy is present, there is an energy present that cannot be produced when you are alone. Synergism says that "the whole is greater than the sum total of its parts." The team that plays as a team wins.

EFFECTIVE TEAM PLAY

Effective teams must have a favorable attitude toward the organization. A favorable climate for interchange must also exist; therefore, hold to informal, comfortable, relaxed, trusting, and cooperative discussions. Avoid judgmental accusations and negative, "that's bad, it won't work" statements.

Keep positive—"That's great, that's good, it could work." To avoid leadership struggles and competition, allow leadership to float. A team needs leadership, not necessarily a leader! Someone should act as the monitor of the discussion to keep it going. Hold to equality, and remember each team member is equally important.

Leadership Styles

A NYTIME LEADERSHIP OR management is mentioned, some-thing needs to be said about the styles of each. Varying styles get differing results. In this chapter I want to give names to two particular styles I encounter that are dominant in most leader/manager cultures.

The first is *protective leadership*. A protective leader is a leader/manager who is only concerned about pleasing the boss and keeping up her reputation among peers. These kinds of leader/managers are political and know how to maneuver within the management culture to protect their jobs and hold a firm position over any "newcomer" or other rival within the organization.

Anytime a new person with skills and talent comes in, pro-tective leaders will do everything not to allow that person to flourish in his or her gifting and will take credit for everything he or she does. This leader/manager will make sure that the threat of this new person taking over the spotlight is diminished by blocking any attempt for them to get on decision-making teams or any possibility for them to get in a place where his/her gifts and abilities are obvious to the boss or other leadership. The end result is that the new person's gifts are neutralized, and he/she eventually gets disheartened and leaves. This is a discouraging environment for all who work there, which minimizes productivity.

The other style is *promotional leadership*. A promotional leader seeks gifted and talented workers and does everything in his power to use the new employee's talent and abilities to the good of the company. This kind of leader/manager has a plan in place to accentuate the strengths of each person in the organization and promote him or her up at any cost to make sure that they are fulfilled and can perform to the maximum of their ability and be the greatest possible benefit to the enterprise.

It is to the benefit of your organization to create positions for excellent and gifted people that might come to work there. Create a new product line, a new service, a new department—anything to take advantage of the strengths a new person brings to the table. When you make room for people to use their creative gifts in the workplace, you will see an explosion in their productivity and an increase in the morale of everyone in the organization. This is a motivational style of leadership that gets the most out of people, while building job satisfaction and personal joy.

When leaders/managers are "protective," they will make leading and managing a business or organization a very difficult and complicated chore. But when leaders/managers are "promotional," they make leading and managing a fulfilling and rewarding job.

Keep Players on the Field

S TANFORD UNIVERSITY SOCIOLOGIST Jeffrey Pfeffer has written a book that nicely blends academic research and practical advice called *Managing With Power: Politics and Influence
in Organizations.*

GAINING THE HIGHEST POSSIBLE COMMITMENT

Pfeffer focuses on techniques to obtain emotional commitment. One obvious way of gaining commitment is to do favors
for others. "I'll scratch your back and then you scratch mine."
It probably works better in reverse. You can build commitment by having others do favors for you! Says Pfeffer:

> If a person complies with my request for a favor, self-
> perception will tend to cause that person to think he
> or she likes me—why do a favor for someone you don't

like? A cycle may begin, in which I do you a small favor, and you feel obliged to repay me. But the very act of your doing something for me helps to commit you to me, and thus further cements the relationship.

Pfeffer cites the case of Jimmy Carter's successful win of the presidency in 1976. His strategy was simple: to build an outsider's campaign and recruit outsiders to run it for you. In 1974, Carter approached Democrats who had lost their primaries and asked for their help. This group became the core of his campaign. As Carter states:

> Contrary to what many people assume, the most effective way to gain a person's loyalty is not to do him or her a favor, but to let that person do one for you.[31]

If you have a great cause that would benefit anyone and everyone involved, then do them a favor by asking them to do you a favor by carrying some of the workload. When you have a plan and they don't, when you provide leadership where there is no other obvious leader, you will find that people will want to follow you.

BEWARE OF THE COMMITMENT KILLERS

To gain the highest possible commitment, you must be able to motivate team players. However, there are actions that may be considered commitment killers.

When there is a *general lack of direction* and it seems that leadership doesn't know where it's going, people bail out. Also, the work must be interesting—boring tasks cause a loss of interest.

People like to know how they are doing and how they can improve; therefore, they need feedback concerning performance. And if they are performing well and want to participate, let them. No one likes to warm the bench all the time. Use everyone.

Leaders must know *what the team needs and give it to them.* People need support from leadership. People will make mistakes and even fail, and when a project fails, no one wants to do it again. This general lack of accomplishment can kill future involvement of team members. Help them overcome the sense of failure with encouragement and training. Keep them in the game.

A team member *does not want to feel that he or she is being isolated from the rest of the staff.* Isolation from activities, meetings, and away trips makes a person feel unwanted. This feeling of rejection can cause him or her to emotionally disconnect from the company or start complaining and criticizing others. Include every person in some collaborative meeting or event.

Openness to new ideas and truth about problem areas are essential to keep everyone involved. The lack of new ideas or acknowledgment of problems erodes the integrity of the enterprise and the faith of the staff.

NEGOTIATING SKILLS—YOU DO IT EVERY DAY

Although *negotiation* may be a rather intimidating word for some people, it may help to know that this is a skill you have already used to some degree—probably many more times than you realize. Whether it's engaging your teenager about the best time for her to be home that night or deciding where the family will go on vacation, you are always negotiating something. How many times have you had to negotiate with the leadership team at the office on decisions that would affect your staff or your ability to do your job satisfactorily? Probably often, so relax and learn from this lesson and from what you already do every day.

How many times have you been in one or more of the following situations?

> ❯ You need to ask your boss for a salary increase.

> ❯ You want to convince a son or daughter to complete a chore he or she may not want to do.

> ❯ You are representing your company in sensitive talks concerning a strategic alliance with another firm.

> You are dealing with city council on a rezoning issue for your business or church.

The stakes may be different in each case, but the common thread running through them is the need for negotiation skills. Negotiating is an activity in which all managers engage to some degree, perhaps dozens of times every day.

Typically negotiation takes place informally: on the telephone, at a short notice meeting, or during an impromptu conversation with someone in the hallway. Sometimes negotiation can take place abruptly, when you are least prepared, and be concluded in a matter of seconds.

Regardless of the form negotiation takes, in order to run your business successfully, it is very important to have a well-developed set of negotiation skills. Even if you feel you already have a talent for negotiating, there are always ways to develop and continuously improve your negotiation skills.

One of the greatest uses of negotiation skills is when you are negotiating on behalf of your company or boss, and your effectiveness will have a positive effect on everyone in the organization. To develop these skills, you should study the art of negotiation and use it often.

Most people, when they think of negotiation, have in mind those rare occasions when people sit at a table and hold intense discussions in some formal way. The major difference between this type of negotiation and other types is the need for planning. Just like in any formal process, negotiation planning is much more structured. In these situations, it is important to:

> Develop an agenda for use in guiding the meeting.

> Define issues, alternatives, and what's in it for them/us.

> Have available an alternate contract if an impasse is reached.

> Have knowledge of the party you are negotiating with.

It is also important to note that this type of negotiation is primarily the exception, not the rule. Most negotiations you will participate in will involve day-to-day operations of your business and will focus more on building long-term relationships than on making a deal. To increase your negotiation skills, you need to increase your awareness of what you are doing and learn to use both your intellect and your intuition during the negotiation process.

The best way to approach negotiation is to be wisely cooperative. That is, look for areas of agreement that can benefit both sides. Of course, it is important to protect your own interests in such a way that you feel satisfied with the outcome of the negotiation.

THE GOOD NEGOTIATOR

Good negotiators understand how to build key relationships, how to identify what people need, how to give them what they need, and how to get what they want in return—all in a way that seems effortless. This is the win-win principle. It is absolutely necessary that both parties walk away with a win. Otherwise there will be no long-term relationship, and you both lose.

As a manager, try to refrain from viewing negotiation as a competitive endeavor in which you have to make a killing in order to emerge the "winner." Indeed, negotiation is best viewed as a stepping stone to forming relationships—with others in your company and with customers, suppliers, and others—that have long-term consequences for your company. In this sense, negotiation never really ends. One piece of negotiation is often the beginning of the next phase of negotiation.

UNDERSTAND THE PERSONALITY

Broadly speaking, there are *two personality types* among managers, and the characteristics of these types can affect the way they negotiate.

Autocratic managers typically hold the view that they are

going to get what they want when they interact with subordinates because their inherent authority precludes the need to negotiate. These managers do not realize that in the process of handing out orders, they are engaged in a kind of one-sided negotiation that can antagonize others, with the result that the tasks they wish to see completed may be carried out improperly or not at all. The more they try to control, the more they lose control of the final outcome.

This type of manager must learn to be more collaborative. Autocratic managers have a tendency to miss the big picture. When these types of managers fail to negotiate effectively, the results of their efforts often suffer. While autocratic types may believe they are skilled negotiators, they often aren't because they lack the ability to listen and to empathize.

The second personality type is the *accommodating manager*. These folks are more concerned with what others want than with their own needs. In order to avoid conflict, they don't negotiate at all and often end up overriding their own interests. Since negotiation implies potential conflict (something these managers avoid at all costs), it is critical for them to take responsibility for forcing a certain amount of compromise. This is the only way they will be able to represent the interests of their company and get the win the company needs in the negotiating process.

If after becoming aware of your personal strengths and weaknesses as a manager you find that you do not feel comfortable negotiating in certain circumstances, it is probably best for you to have someone else negotiate on your behalf.

NEGOTIATION AND VARIETY

It is critical to understand that negotiating cannot be learned by following a prepackaged set of principles and applying them to all situations. That would work if everyone could be counted on to behave rationally and predictably, but they can't because people are often emotional and irrational. To negotiate well, you must be prepared to use a variety of approaches.

The good news is that like anything else, negotiation gets easier the more you do it. With practice, you will develop your own personal style and become comfortable with your own limits. As in so many other things in life, experience is the best teacher when it comes to effective negotiations.

Conflict Resolution—Disagreeing Agreeably

Disputes will occur more often than we are ready to deal with them, but deal with them we must. Hardly a leadership meeting goes by without one or two conflicts. In the majority of cases, conflicts will be resolved before the meeting is adjourned. How do we resolve conflicts without making enemies of our peers? What happens if conflicts go unresolved? In order to be successful, managers *must* be great peacemakers with skills for resolving conflicts. Here's how:

1. Separate people from the problem.

It is critical to address problems, not personalities, and to avoid the tendency to attack your opponent personally. If the other person feels threatened, he will defend his self-esteem and make attacking the *real problem* more difficult. Try to maintain a rational, goal-oriented frame of mind. If your opponent attacks you personally, don't let him hook you into an emotional reaction. Let him blow off steam without taking it personally, and try to understand the problem behind the aggression.

Make sure to send signals that you know the conflict is about the issues at hand and isn't personal. This will help to prevent the other side from getting defensive.

2. Identify the real problem.

A key element of finding common interests is *problem identification*. It is important to define the problem in a way that is mutually acceptable to both sides. This involves depersonalizing the problem so as not to raise the defensiveness of the other person. Thus, an employee discussing a problem with the boss is likely to be more effective if he defines the problem as "I need to understand the issues better" or "I don't see where I missed the recommended actions here," rather than "You didn't show me how this worked" or "How did you expect me to do it right?"

3. Discover underlying interests.

We need to be very clear about our interests, which may not be as easy as it would appear. Equally important is the need to find out the other person's key interests. It is impossible to resolve an issue if you don't know what interests the other party has at stake. You may be withholding something from them that is insignificant to your interests.

We are used to identifying our own interests, but a critical element in negotiation is to understand the other person's underlying interests and needs as well. By probing and exchanging information we can find the commonalities between us and minimize the differences that seem to be evident.

It is also important to realize that conflict that requires resolution is neither good nor bad. There can be positive and negative outcomes. It can be destructive, but it can also play a productive role for you personally and in your relationships—both personal and professional. The important point is to manage the conflict, not to suppress it, and not to let conflict escalate out of control. That is why we must know what interests are at stake. Many of us seek to avoid conflict, but many times we should use conflict as a critical aspect of creativity and motivation.

4. Hear the person out.

Until you let the other person say what she wants to say, you cannot begin to resolve her issues. Don't assume you know the answer before you give the person a chance to explain the problem in her own words.

> ❯ Let the other person "vent," acknowledge his views, listen actively, find areas you can immediately agree with, and make small concessions. Reduce tension

through humor. Don't take his venting personally, and don't get angry.

> Increase the accuracy of communication, listen closely in the middle of conflict, rephrase the other's comments to make sure you understand them, and get her to repeat confusing statements.

> Break issues down into controllable pieces. Don't try to solve huge all-encompassing issues all at once. This will unnecessarily bring others into the conflict.

> Find common interests and goals—since conflict tends to magnify perceived differences and minimize similarities, look for greater common goals (we are in this together); find a common enemy; focus on what you have in common.

> Focus on a clear understanding of the other's needs, and figure out ways to move toward them. Don't let your position be too much of a factor.

> Try your best to say yes when you can. You can do this when you attach appropriate conditions that must be met first. *Ask the person to* restate his/her demands, repackage his/her grievance, offer a win-win compromise, emphasize the positives, and state his/her bottom-line request. It may be simpler than you think. Sometimes the person's win-win offer is easier to accommodate than the one you were thinking of.

> Settle the issue and get the person's agreement. Once you have reached a solution, write it down and get all parties to sign off on it. It may need to be adjusted, but at least you have areas of agreement to work from the next time around.

21

Strategic Alliances

A STRATEGIC ALLIANCE IS a relationship that has the potential to contribute significantly and in multiple ways to the growth of your business and every internal and external activity of the enterprise. Such partnerships are a cornerstone of Cisco System's growth strategy. More than 10 percent of the company's revenues in fiscal year 2002 (more than $2 billion) derived from Cisco's strategic alliance relationships.

> What all this alliance activity reflects is business executives' perception that the corporate world has never appeared as hostile, bewildering, and unstable as it does today.[32]
>
> —JOHN HARBISON AND PETER PEKAR

Understand the potential of building an alliance versus starting a new area or department within your company. In other

152

words, calculate when to build a solution in-house, when to buy into one that already exists, and when to create an alliance or partnership. When you decide to "partner" with a company that is already in existence, choose the best partner. You get immediate credibility when you partner with companies that have had long-term success and have earned the respect of the community. This helps put you in a better position and gives you recognition as well as a piece of the influence enjoyed by the other company.

By strategically aligning yourself with excellent organizations, you get the best-in-class capabilities. For example, you don't have to do the work of identifying the skills needed, hiring the right people, building a solid management system, and having strong operations when you partner with a business that already does this well.

So choose the partner to build a strategic alliance with, one with proven long-term results that can strengthen your weaknesses. And make sure you have something to offer—it must be a win-win situation.

The advantages of strategic alliances are many. You gain new relationships, increase your influence, and leap-frog the learning curve in some instances. What may take you years to learn is already part of someone else's bank of knowledge and experience, from which you can benefit immediately. Doing it all by yourself is not the goal. The goal is doing more than you can do by yourself. Concentrate on making the pie bigger rather than on worrying about your slice.

Partnering with some other organization can also help the company you manage break inertia and get big MO on the field. Momentum is the key to remaining successful in a highly competitive world. One species of Chinese bamboo takes four years to sprout, then grows ninety feet in six months. Sometimes you seem to languish for years before you leap toward success. Strategic alliances can help make that happen sooner.

22

The Joseph Journey

JOSEPH WAS IN every respect a great leader and, as Scripture reveals, a great manager on behalf of Pharaoh and the nation of Egypt. In Joseph's story we can see many events we can relate to. Joseph's life experience is typical of many our own experiences. In a completely different setting and time and circumstances, we can trace our own struggles from the prison to the palace. In this chapter, I want to draw some analogies from Joseph's journey and make application to what many of us have gone through or are going through. This could be your "Joseph journey."

THE DREAM

As a child, did you dream of being the greatest baseball player of all time? Maybe you dreamed of becoming the heavyweight champion of the world, Miss America, or a scientist.

What was your dream?

Something big is in all of our futures. We dream of being a rock star, singing to tens of thousands in a packed auditorium, but in real life that dream may be interpreted as being the leader of thousands of employees as the president of a Fortune 500 company. We may dream of leading the Boston Celtics to the NBA championship. This could be a dream that turns into an entrepreneurial success story. It is a dream…your dream…a dream of doing something significant, something out of the ordinary, something great. How it will be interpreted by your life's events is uncertain, but it is still your dream, and it will come to pass if you don't give up.

Joseph's dream of the stars and the moon bowing down to him was eventually interpreted as his family coming to him to buy food to prevent them from starving. Joseph had risen to the position of ruler over Egypt—the great star over Egypt—and had it within his power to help or turn away anyone who came to him. His dreams of sheaves in the fields bowing down to his sheaf was interpreted when he recognized his brothers as his family as they bowed down to him trying to gain his favor, not knowing that Joseph was not dead, but very much alive…and in this case, in charge. Joseph wept when he saw his brothers and ran out of their presence so as not to be detected for who he was. The emotion was overwhelming because he realized all at once why his life took the turn of events it did and that his dream had actually come true.

THE DREAM KILLER

As a boy, I had many dreams. I was Elvis, Muhammad Ali… I was rich and famous, a great football player. Like many of the kids I grew up with, I had aspirations for greatness. I didn't have a clue what it all meant, what it would cost me, or what the interpretation would be, but I dreamed and dreamed. From Superman capes to slicked back hair and guitars, there wasn't anything that I didn't dream of becoming.

Then the dream killer came.

In my school days, during the late fifties and early sixties, we had elementary school from first to sixth grade. After that came junior high. Wow! Junior high. This is where you no longer had just one teacher but changed rooms every hour to a new subject and teacher. You left on a bus early in the morning, went across town, and didn't come back till the end of the day. This is where it all started to count. It was a bit scary, but it was reality—I was going to junior high.

My grades were decent in elementary school. I was in advanced math and on occasion would run up to nearly making straight A's. Notice that I said "nearly." School was not my thing. Homework was out of the question, and with six rambunctious kids, Mama couldn't keep up with all of us. So I got by with little effort. I knew that seventh grade was coming and that I would really start trying once junior high became my place of study. In the meantime, girls and football seemed to be enough to keep me busy.

It was the end of sixth grade, and my teacher was handing out report cards. It was my turn to get my final report card, my final word of encouragement from my teacher, and then wait for the summer to end so I could begin a new stage in my life. As I approached the teacher's desk, he looked at me with a stern face and said these unfortunate words: "Hornsby, you will never make it!"

What did he mean by that? I thought. It was like someone tried to punch me in the nose and I was working to dodge the blow. *Never make it? Oh well.* I went home, gave the report card to Mama, and told her, "You know what my teacher said when he gave me my report card? He said, 'Hornsby, you will never make it.'"

Mama just brushed it off. "Really? Oh, Billy... just forget it," she said. And that was it. *Just forget it.* The problem was... I never forgot it.

When I finally got to seventh grade—and for the next twelve

years—I stopped dreaming. With every dream and with every failure came the words, "You will never make it." If I failed a test or missed a pass from the quarterback, I heard the words over and over again. Those words would follow me into my marriage, in every job failure, every day, every year. "You will never make it" became a state of being. Subconsciously I allowed it to dictate my actions and my thoughts. I was on the road to a dreamless life of failure, the road to nowhere.

But dreams come true…even with dream killers around.

At age twenty-four, I became a Christian. For the first time I understood that failure did not have to be the foundation I built my life on. With forgiveness, not only of moral failure but of every other miscue, God was giving me a new start, a chance to overcome my past. This all came to a head at an interview pertaining to a battery of tests I took for my employer at that time. It was a great turn of events.

"Manager Trainee" was the title of the position I held with a large drugstore chain. They had sent trainees from all over the state to take some tests being administered by an industrial psychologist. It was two days of intensive test taking, round-table negotiations of mock business transactions, and tons of personal evaluation interviews and questions. When it was all over, we took turns going into the room where we got our final "report card." My turn came, and this upbeat man in his early forties looked at me and said. "Mr. Hornsby, you are not going to be with this company very long."

What else is new…? I thought. *You'll never make it* came back to me so quickly! I answered him, "That doesn't surprise me, but why do you say that?"

His answer changed my life and broke the chains the words my sixth-grade teacher had spoken over me. "I have given this test to thousands of people around the country, and you have made the highest score of anyone that I have ever tested. The reason I said you won't be with this company long is that this company does not have enough to offer you." The next thing he said changed my life for good. *"I don't know what you will end up doing, but whatever it is, you will be successful!"*

When that psychologist said those words, I knew the origin. It wasn't just him talking. Somehow God was saying to me, "The words of your sixth-grade teacher will no longer affect you. From now on, you will not fail but rather succeed."

What an impact this interview had on my life! I remember getting up from the table and calling my brother Frank before I left the building. "Frank, I want to tell you what just happened." I relayed the story of the years of being under the power of the negative, dream-killing words of my teacher and what had just happened in this psychologist's office. "Frank, God has just reversed the curse!"

With that, my whole life changed…I started dreaming again.

Ray Charles has been able to do what few musicians can—create music that appeals to young and old, black and white, rich and poor. He successfully crossed major boundaries.

Charles lost both parents and a brother before he was grown. He grew up in a school for the blind, where he learned to play piano and sing. By his late teens, he was a hit in central and north Florida. His friends believed in his talent, and Charles believed in them. In 1946, when Lucky Millinder's band arrived in Orlando, Charles managed to get an audition. It was his first chance at the big time.

Charles sang and played with all his might. Millinder listened quietly. At the end of the audition, as Charles expected to hear praise, all he heard was silence and then finally these devastating words, "Ain't good enough, kid." Charles thought he had heard incorrectly and asked Millinder to repeat what he had said. "You heard me. You don't got what it takes." Charles later said of the incident, "I went back to my room and cried for days."

In retrospect, Charles considered that blow to be the "best thing that ever happened to me. After I got over feeling sorry for myself, I went back and started practicing, so nobody would ever say that about me again."[33]

Stop now and re-dream your dream. What was it that was so exciting, so worthwhile, that you thrilled at the thought of it? What made you jump out of bed and run to meet the new day with hope and expectation? What was it? When you recall that great dream, you must hold on to it. This dream will become your source of inspiration to go on and accomplish the great thing God created you to do. When it happens, you will know that it is your dream coming true. It may not be the rock star scenario, but it will be interpreted and it will be significant. It will be a major accomplishment, and you will know that your dream has come true. You are going to make it!

DESPISED

Joseph was despised for his dreams. You may be despised for yours. Society has many more failures than successes. More businesses fail than succeed. The same is true of churches and the best thought-out plans. So when you come up with some bright idea about having great success, be ready to be resisted, rejected, and ridiculed. Most people have failed and aren't really excited about your success. Even your family and best friends may think you're crazy and a little too radical.

Though dreams are despised by most "reality thinkers," dreams possess the energy and the stuff that brings joy and fulfillment in life. The reality is that most people fail and don't mind a bit if you do, too. Not only do they expect you to fail, but also secretly they would like to see you fail. Knowing this helps you adjust your attitude about their attitude . . . it doesn't matter what they think.

Of course, it is wise to think realistically, to count the costs and weigh your options. But it is not always clear where your dreams will take you or where they will be fulfilled. You should use the wisdom God gave you and the counsel of wise men and women, but the decision is still yours. Look for signs of hope during times of resistance, and hold on to your dream during times of ridicule.

BETRAYED

Who hasn't been betrayed at some time in his or her life? It seems that whenever we launch out to accomplish something meaningful, there is always someone in our life, or on the team, or a co-owner in the company who will betray us. It could be the jealous staffperson who always makes innuendos about your honesty or performance to the boss, or the competitive peer who wants the promotion you are in line for. Whoever it is, betrayal is part of the journey.

Once you realize that around some turn on the journey you will be betrayed, be ready to deal with it. Learn whom you can trust, what information you should be sparing with—that could be the way you are guided to your destiny.

ENSLAVED

Joseph was sold into slavery for his dreams. He ended up in Potiphar's house as a servant. Though he was a slave, his dream eventually bought his freedom.

How can you enslave a dream? When you know in your heart that someday you will achieve your goal and accomplish your purpose, nothing can prevent you. You must look at every trial, every failure and setback as mere stepping stones to success…not to your tombstone. You may be out of the picture right now, your hopes dashed, your network unraveled, but you are still here, pressing on to the final outcome, which is sure to be in your favor. Your integrity and faithfulness will keep you in the game.

Persistence and diligence will pay off. Your struggle in the face of danger will only make you more determined to overcome the obstacles before you. This next story is a great example of how we should look at trials. Know your destiny and view every situation in the light of that destiny.

The story is told of an organization out west that offered a bounty of five thousand dollars for each wolf captured alive. Sam and Jed decided this was a great deal. They saw a tremendous opportunity to strike it rich, just as their prospecting ancestors of old had done. So they outfitted themselves for the challenge and hiked into the area. For weeks, they spent day and night scouring the mountains and forests in search of their valuable prey.

Late one night, exhausted, they fell asleep and began to dream of their potential fortune. Sam suddenly awoke with a start and rubbed his eyes. He wasn't entirely sure if he was awake or dreaming, but then realized that, indeed, he was awake. At the edges of the light cast by their campfire, he saw that he and Jed were surrounded by about fifty wolves—each with flaming eyes and bared teeth. He nudged his friend to awaken him, crying, "Jed, wake up! We're rich!"[34]

Accused

Accusations are the bitter arrows of dishonest people who are themselves guilty of offense. In offices around the world and in every business enterprise, accusations are thrown around like darts so that people can dodge the guilt and blame for personal and moral failure. It is the pin-the-tail-on-the-donkey scenario of people who can't take responsibility for their mistakes and lack of character. When accusations happen, it hurts, sometimes for a long time. Just like Potiphar's wife, guilty of seducing an innocent man, she accused Joseph of the crime she wanted to commit, a crime he was innocent of.

Ultimately, if you dream big dreams you will be accused and convicted for dreaming. I am writing this to tell you that it's all right! Keep dreaming! You will overcome accusations sooner or later and will be back on track toward your destiny.

Imprisoned

You can throw me in prison, but you can't lock up my dream. Many famous and infamous people have been imprisoned for their dreams—only to come out and accomplish their outstanding or outlandish objectives.

An imprisoned dream is like an expensive bottle of wine—it just gets better with age. In Joseph's case, imprisonment provided him with a few more years of experience in leadership and the wisdom that goes along with it. It was a time of building character to prepare for the task he would be given. It may be the same for you. You may feel imprisoned in your current position. Just keep a learner's attitude. It may be the maturing process you are going through now that will spell success for you later.

Major James Nesmeth, an average weekend golfer shooting in the mid- to low nineties, dreamed of improving his golf game. But then for seven years he never touched a club or set foot on a fairway. During those years, however, he developed an amazingly effective technique for improving his game. The first time he returned to a course, he shot an astonishing seventy-four! He had cut twenty strokes off his average.

What was his secret? Visualization. For those seven years, Major Nesmeth was a prisoner of war in North Vietnam. He was imprisoned in a cage four and one-half feet high and five feet long. Most of those years he saw no one, talked to no one, and had no physical activity. He knew he had to find some way to occupy his mind or he would lose his sanity, so he began to visualize playing golf. Each day he played a full eighteen holes at the imaginary country club of his dreams. He imagined every detail, every shot. And not once did he miss a shot or a putt. Seven days a week, four hours a day, he played eighteen holes in his mind.[35]

Chuck Colson has thoughts about the word *success*. Before the Watergate scandal, he was an American success story. From scholarships to courtroom victories, to serving as special counsel to the president, he was regarded as a very successful man. Now he shares with thousands of prisoners in their prison cells all over the nation. Yes, he was successful, but one day, while speaking to some hopeless prisoners in Delaware, after one of them thanked him for his work, Colson realized that he was finally seeing success from God's point of view. He wrote, "The real legacy of my life was my biggest failure, that I was an ex-convict. Only when I lost everything I thought made Chuck Colson a great guy had I found the true self God intended me to be.... My greatest humiliation—being sent to prison—was the beginning of God's greatest use of my life."[36]

FORGOTTEN

It's amazing to me that great people who do great things are so easily forgotten. Do you remember Mark McGwire? He was the first person to beat Roger Maris's thirty-seven-year-old home run record by hitting an astounding seventy home runs in one season. He was a daily television headline, hamburger ad spokesperson, and American hero. But after the 1998 season, it seemed like he couldn't hit another home run. He and Sammy Sosa, two great rivals, seemed to cool off so much that there was nothing newsworthy to report about them. The media tried to get them to trash each other, but they had too much character to do that, so the media just stopped the stories. Then came Barry Bonds, seventy-three homers in the 2001 season. Bonds had become the new poster child for Major League Baseball. McGwire was put on the back shelf, forgotten.

McGwire now has started the Mark McGwire Foundation for Children. He also works with the National Kidney Foundation to help kids deal with bed-wetting. He has committed his life to serving the less fortunate. But in the sports arena he is practically a forgotten hero.

This story is repeated thousands of times every decade. Our heroes disappear from our radar screens, their good deeds mostly forgotten. Think of the bravery of men and women around the world during wartime, disasters, and national crises. There are monuments around our landscape to remind us, but we forget. It is human nature.

Can you remember all you did for the organizations you worked for or even work for now? Think of the sacrifices you have made to make your boss and the company successful. How many days of family fun and pleasure did you give up for the sake of the success of your business? Now all of that is forgotten in the past. It is so easy for past deeds to drop into obscurity. Joseph's good deed to the king's servants was also forgotten... until the most opportune moment.

REMEMBERED

Good deeds, heroic acts, and selfless acts have a way of resurfacing just when you need them to. In these times of reflection, what will stand out the most are the good deeds we have done. Good deeds and sacrifices are never done in vain. Wait for the moment of discovery—it is coming. Your dreams will be brought to light. What you did for others will sooner or later be remembered. Increase the likelihood of being remembered by doing good things for people.

ENLIGHTENED

Here was Joseph's great enlightenment: "Joseph interpreted the king's dream." Joseph's experience, his integrity, and the "divine spirit" working in him gave him the revelation he needed to lift him from bondage to bounty, from the prison to the palace. What will be your enlightenment?

For me, enlightenment came when I realized what my greatest, most dominant gift was. I didn't have to take a test to find out what it was—people told me. The same is true with most people. Others tell them what they are good and gifted at. We must listen in order to discover our gifts.

Just as Joseph must have realized that he possessed the ability to rule well, many of us come to the realization that we are really good at something. Something we do is easy for us and we excel. You need to acknowledge this to yourself. This is not boasting, because you know many people who are much better than you are, but you are gifted in an area that will bring you success in that realm. Stay focused on that gift because you are unique, and try to improve it.

Your gift may be the ability to read financial statements and understand the financial history of a company's profit and loss record. For others, it may be the ability to troubleshoot problems and find solutions. For still others, it may be the ability to work behind the scenes and make the boss more successful.

As I began to realize what my gift was, I focused on making it better. The more I used it, the more it worked for me. My dominant gift became the key to my success in every aspect of what I did for the organization, for the number one, and for myself. It created influence for me, increased my financial income, and gave me a deep sense of satisfaction and fulfillment. Your dominant gift will do the same for you. Discover it and improve it—it could be your enlightenment.

RESTORED

Once Joseph exercised his gift to the delight of the king, the king restored Joseph's freedoms and restored his respectability. Restoration is the act of being reestablished—in this case, to fulfill what was intended for you. Joseph was now on course to complete his purpose in life…to fulfill his destiny.

Sometimes it feels as if we are languishing in the background, unnoticed, and as if we are losing at the game of success. No one acknowledges us, and we feel like we're on the treadmill of life. We're in the rut of mere existence and are digging a hole deeper and more difficult to climb out of. Finally, someone takes note of our gifting, our value to the enterprise and the cause, and we are restored to a place of visible service.

In this place of visible service, we are given the chance to display all our gifts to the benefit of everyone involved and to the bottom line of the organization, whatever that bottom line is. We are now in the position to serve with our gifts and make a difference in the world. We delight in the opportunity to do what we have dreamed of doing…and we will do it. We will not blow it!

Empowered

Pharaoh had his servants bring Joseph a clean change of clothes. He put his signet ring on Joseph's finger, his royal robe on Joseph's back, and set him in the second chariot. Once Joseph was restored, he was empowered. The signet ring was Pharaoh's stamp, the equivalent of his signature. His robe was his royalty and authority, and these were given to Joseph to use as though he were king.

When we are empowered to do something significant, we must understand the position we are put in. First of all, empowerment must be viewed not just as a personal promotion, but as promotion of the enterprise. It is the enterprise you work for, not for your personal riches and success, but for the increase of both the riches and the success of everyone in the endeavor. In other words, it is your opportunity to make a meaningful contribution to whole enterprise, not just to sweeten your pot.

We must view empowerment as a chance to count for something bigger than ourselves. Just as Joseph used his empowerment to save Egypt and his family, we must use times of empowerment to make a difference in others' lives. After having been empowered, will you be able to say, "I made a difference," "I furthered the cause," "I made a difference in someone's life for the good," "I cooperated, created, empowered, embraced, and finished what I was put on earth to do"? This is your chance to bring unimaginable success to your superiors. Through his empowerment from the king, Joseph made him far richer than Pharaoh had ever imagined.

The most fulfilling thing we can do in life is to be a significant factor in the success of someone else. Empower someone!

Reunited

At the end of Joseph's story we find him reunited with his family. Now, this represents not only the coming together of his kinfolk, but also Joseph's reunion with his dream—the dream of being great on behalf of his family.

When we are reunited with our dreams as we travel our own Joseph journey, we must realize that we have come full circle and are given the opportunity to do what we always dreamed of doing. This is not the fulfillment of what we wanted to accomplish, but rather the chance to live our dream and begin the work of accomplishing our goals. Now that we have the chance to live out our dreams, we begin to refocus and gear up for the challenges that lie ahead. There will be struggles, but the struggles are for what we always thought our life was meant for. The struggles are worth it when we are living our dream.

FORGIVE

I can think of only a few things that could kill a dream. Hate, dishonesty, and greed are a few. Retaliation is a surefire spoiler. Had Joseph retaliated against his brothers, I really don't think he would be mentioned in the Holy Scriptures. He would have passed into history as yet another person who failed to discern how to live out his dream. Joseph saw the fear on their faces when he revealed his identity to his brothers, yet he forgave them for it all. In the name of a greater cause, Joseph was willing to let the injustices of the past be forgiven. This is what he said: "You meant evil against me, but God meant it for good in order to bring about this present result, to preserve many people alive" (Genesis 50:20).

Can you see the greater good, the better purpose for your life, rather than to settle the score with those who worked against you or envied you? Will you use the glory of the moment for striking back—use your energy for doing what is profitable for vengeance—or will you see the higher calling, a greater utilization of your position? Will you be able to overlook personal injury and see the opportunity for healing?

If you can, you will realize your dream.

DELIVER THE DREAM

Remember that Joseph's dream was not to become rich or to lord his power over his family, but rather to be in a position to deliver them from starvation. The wealth and power was the interpretation of his dream. *Dreams are not delivered to us, but given to us to deliver to others.*

Remember, there is a bigger picture here. Christ is in the physical lineage of Jacob, Joseph's father. Christ comes directly from Judah, Joseph's brother. How big a picture is that? Can you see beyond your immediate circumstances and envision what your dream could mean in the future?

When we reach our place of empowerment, we must realize that it is a place of delivering our dream to the people we live with and the enterprise we work for. When we reach a place of influence and power, the purpose is not to wield power, but to dispense power. Our position of leadership is not there so that we can gain followers, but so we can build leaders. And finally, when we start living our dream, we should begin helping other people fulfill their dreams.

There are thousands of stories of men who finally strike it rich twenty years into their marriage, and during that time, the wife had to sacrifice for her husband's education and training—only to have him dump her to live out his dream with someone else. This sounds so cruel—and it is—but we often do the same thing to people who helped make our dreams come true. When we reach our highest and most noble goals, our success will ultimately be measured by how many people we brought with us to share in it.

The End Result

DURING JOSEPH'S SERVICE to Pharaoh, he enjoyed unimaginable success. Not only did he save the nations from starvation, but through his management skill, the years of plenty and resulting harvest during the years of famine, he amassed a fortune for Pharaoh. He collected money by selling the grain, then all the cattle, then all the land. Not only this, but he distributed seed for the people to sow new crops and had them pay one-fifth, or 20 percent, of their increase to Pharaoh for as long as they lived. He did all of this for Pharaoh. This is a successful subordinate leader/manager.

YOUR JOSEPH JOURNEY

What about *your* Joseph journey? Where are you on your way to fulfilling your dream? Learn from the lessons of this chapter, and prepare for all the great things that await you in life.

You may wonder, *What about a promotion to number one? When will my day come?*

Some people are destined to become the primary leader. Be ready to step up and take the lead position. Many second in commands don't move up to lead chariot quickly because of their inability to prepare themselves accordingly. If you do, that's great, but you must have selected, trained, and developed the person who will take over your role as second chariot and do as good as or a better job than you. Have that person mentored and ready for the task so that when the time comes, a delay doesn't occur.

So how will you lead? Is it clear in your mind how you would take the organization to the next level? Do you know how you would add value to the employees or reorganize them for maximum productivity and reward? There are hundreds of questions that you need to answer. But the main one is this: "How will you lead?"

Below is what I call my "Leadership Point of View." It has helped me keep my eyes on important issues and stay consistent. It has given me something to fall back on when things get cloudy. Put your own ideas into it, and build your own point of view as a leader.

THE LEADERSHIP POINT OF VIEW

What is your leadership point of view? What do you believe about leadership? You may have read scores of books on leadership, but how do you implement what you read on a consistent basis?

"Having a point of view is worth 50 IQ points," said Roger Enrico, CEO of PepsiCo.[37]

Consider the following acrostic, which reveals my personal leadership point of view, and then sit down and write your own.

LEADERSHIP

L—Love what you do and those with whom you work.

You may ask, "What does love have to do with leadership?" Love never fails! How would you like to have the promise of constant success? Then love what you do and the people you work with. Love is kind...is patient...seeks not its own...bears all things...believes all things...hopes all things! What promises success more than that?

E—Encourage others to be their best, and help them improve.

To encourage is to "inspire with courage, confidence, and hope." The people who follow you are in need of constant encouragement. One of the most important roles I play in the lives of those I lead is to tell them, "You can do it!" If they can't do it, then get them the training and instruction to help them become more proficient and useful. You will build lifelong skills in those that you encourage and equip.

A—Add value to people's lives through affirmation and training.

The key element that adds value to our lives is knowing that we were created by God. But what if you feel inadequate as a provider for your family, or useless in your job? What can be done to increase people's worth to themselves and to others? First, speak positively to them about the good things they possess, their gifts. Then give the opportunity to learn through instruction and practical experience, which will help them grow personally. As leaders we have been given stewardship over "human capital," to make each person more valuable to him- or herself and to the community they work and live in.

D—Delegate responsibilities to others in order to develop their skills.

Trust those you lead enough to give them the responsibility of doing tasks you normally reserve for yourself. This gives them the practical experience they will need to lead. When we entrust people with the "important" jobs, we communicate to them that we have confidence in them.

Delegation not just a way to get rid of necessary tasks, but it develops people and new skills. You must maintain the responsibility of the task until it is completed. In the meantime, there are always other more important things that you need to be doing.

I have discovered that others on my staff can do many of my tasks better. "I am; therefore, I delegate!"

E—Exemplify the type of leader you want others to become.

You serve as the example of how things should be done and with what attitude they should be done. Others will follow your example as you serve as their role model. If you do things that you don't want replicated, change! This keeps the pressure on me to be, in every area of my leadership, the model that I should be.

R—Respect everyone.

Hold in high esteem everyone in your organization and family. We have a tendency to favor those who agree with us and think less of those who disagree. This is a character flaw. We must honor people on the basis that they belong to God. The "least among us" deserve the utmost respect. When you respect others, you will honor them and uphold their position and reputation to others.

S—Serve those that serve you and the organization.

Meet the needs of those in your organization. As each of us works to meet the other's needs, as we serve in the organization, we make each person's job easier and more pleasant. In reality, there is no positional or intellectual hierarchy, only lesser or greater degrees of servants.

H—Humble yourself by thinking more highly of others.
Bring down your personal status or rank in your own eyes, and lift up other people. This is accomplished when you give up the "perks" associated with positions of higher importance. Come to understand your dependence on others for your success. Let them know that you're where you are because they allow you to stand on their shoulders.

I—"I may not have the best idea."
One of the subtlest errors we make in self-appraisal is thinking that we always know what's best. Not listening to the counsel of the "least" will cost us the most. I have personally discovered over the years that my staff always has valuable input that helps me make better decisions. I listen carefully to their ideas because I respect their experience and insights.

P—Practice what you say you value—your priorities.
No matter what you say, what you do speaks volumes more to the people with whom you work. I hear it constantly: "I heard what they said, but I'll wait and see if they really do it." As leaders, we must "flesh out" what we preach to others, or we will look like hypocrites. We need to build our values by living out our ideals as much as possible. Then others will take us seriously when we begin to lead them.

In Conclusion

Don't wait to be great; be great now. If you serve as a second in command, be the best that you can be in that position, and make as many other people successful as you can.

Notes

1. Web site www.motivation-tools.com (accessed September 29, 2005).

2. Benedetto, Richard. "Cheney's feet solidly planted in No. 2 spot." *USA TODAY.* January 20, 2005. A.6.

3. Web site http://www.brainyquote.com/quotes/quotes/h/henryford131621.html (accessed September 29, 2005).

4. Web site http://www.brainyquote.com/quotes/authors/a/abraham_maslow.html (accessed September 29, 2005).

5. Lee A. Iacocca, *Iacocca, An Autobiography* (New York: Bantam Books, 1984).

6. Web site http://www.brainyquote.com/quotes/quotes/a/abrahamlin109274.html (accessed September 29, 2005).

7. Michael E. Gerber, *The E-Myth: Why Most Small Businesses Don't Work and What to Do About It,* (Cambridge, MA: Ballinger Publishing Company, 1985).

8. Web site http://www.brainyquote.com/quotes/authors/h/henry_ford.html (accessed September 29, 2005).

9. Web site http://www.brainyquote.com/quotes/authors/v/vincent_van_gogh.html (accessed September 29, 2005).

10. Ibid.

11. Web site http://www.jhu.edu/~gazette/julsep97/sep2297/starr.html (accessed September 29, 2005).

12. Web site http://www.brainyquote.com/quotes/authors/j/john_wooden.html (accessed September 29, 2005).

13. Billy Hornsby, *101 Rules for Relationship* (Billy Hornsby Ministries, 2002), "Rule #37."

14. Web site http://www.brainyquote.com/quotes/authors/m/mark_twain.html (accessed September 29, 2005).

15. Web site http://www.brainyquote.com/quotes/authors/

d/denis_waitley.html (accessed September 29, 2005).

16. Web site http://www.brainyquote.com/quotes/authors/p/peter_f_drucker.html (accessed September 29, 2005).

17. Web site http://www.any-book-in-print.com/desk_signs/coach_1_ds.htm (accessed September 29, 2005).

18. Ibid. *101 Rules for Relationship*, "Rule #7."

19. Rosanne Badowski, *Managing Up* (New York: Currency-Doubleday, 2003).

20. Web site http://cecl.nl.edu/public/issues/dl_spring2004.pdf (accessed September 29, 2005).

21. Ibid. *101 Rules for Relationship*, "Rule #35."

22. James S. Hewett, ed., *Illustrations Unlimited* (Wheaton, IL: Tyndale, 1988), 57.

23. Jim Collins, *Good to Great: Why Some Companies Make the Leap and Others Don't* (Collins, 2001).

24. Allan Cohen, "Leading From the Middle: Issues and Answers on Leadership for Middle Managers," http://www.babsoninsight.com/contentmgr/showdetails.php/id/594 (accessed September 5, 2005).

25. Some material from this chapter partially from an article by Michael Useem, "Leading From the Middle," *Executive Update Online*, October 2002, www.gwsae.org/executiveupdate/2002/october/leading.htm (accessed September 5, 2005).

26. Web site http://www.gwsae.org/executiveupdate/2002/October/leading.htm (accessed September 29, 2005).

27. Web site http://www.motivational-inspirational-corner.com/getquote.html?categoryid=66 (accessed September 29, 2005).

28. Web site http://www.faithfulhope.com/readingroom/item.cfm?doc_id=6548 (accessed September 29, 2005).

29. Web site http://en.thinkexist.com/quotation/for_the_strength_of_the_pack_is_the_wolf-and_the/174800.html (accessed September 29, 2005).

30. Web site http://www.evolutiondeceit.com/chapter20.

php (accessed September 29, 2005).

31. *Managing With Power: Politics and Influence in Organizations*, (Cambridge, MA: Harvard Business School Press, 1994.)

32. John R. Harbison and Peter Pekar, Jr., *Smart Alliances* (Indianapolis, IN: Jossey-Bass, 1998).

33. B. Eugene Griessman, *The Achievement Factors* (New York: Dodd, Mead & Co., 1987), 54–55.

34. Craig Brian Larson, *Illustrations for Preaching and Teaching* (Grand Rapids, MI: Baker Books, 1993), 12.

35. Jack Canfield and Mark Victor Hansen, *A Second Helping of Chicken Soup for the Soul* (Deerfield Beach, FL: Health Communications, 1996), 235–236.

36. Charles Colson, *Loving God* (Grand Rapids, MI: Zondervan Publishing House, 1983, 1987), 21–25.

37. Web site http://www.mydas.com/main.htm+roger+enr ico+IQ+points.html (accessed September 29, 2005).

To Contact the Author

E-mail: billyhornsby@comcast.net

For more information about books and other offers by Billy
Hornsby, please visit the following Web sites:
www.billyhornsby.com
www.101rules.com
www.thankthecrew.com

Other Books by Billy Hornsby:
The Cell Church
Christian Core Values
101 Rules for Relationships
Permission Evangelism